CHICORA
Lost on Lake Michigan

There are a handful of Great Lakes shipwrecks that are familiar even to those with only a passing knowledge of nautical history. This would include the **Griffin**, the very first known wreck in 1679; the **Edmund Fitzgerald**, one of the most recent; the **Carl D. Bradley**, lost near the Manitou Islands in 1958; the tragedy of the **Noronic** at Toronto in 1949, the **Alpena**, which disappeared with all hands in 1880, the **Eastland** which capsized in the Chicago River in 1915 and a few others.

The **Chicora** is one of these.

One circumstance that piqued interest in the **Chicora**, both at the time of the event and later in history, was the development of the telegraph to the point where the loss could be treated as a breaking news story. Newspapers as far away as New York City received the latest information by wire. The news was seldom more than a day old and some of the discoveries had occurred within the hour.

When events were happening quickly the newspapers, especially the hometown papers in St. Joseph and Benton Harbor, Michigan, published extra editions. On one particularly newsworthy day the *Benton Harbor Palladium* issued three "extras" in six hours.

The result was an outpouring of information, misinformation, conjecture and human-interest anecdotes that kept the newspapers churning out front page stories for more than two weeks and features at least annually for the next century.

Fueling the wires and adding interest to the tragedy was the feeling that the boat had not foundered unnoticed in mid-lake, but had come within sight and earshot of the shore during her struggle. As the January 30, 1895, issue of the *Buchanan Record* observed:

> It is one thing to read of shipwrecks on distant waters and quite another to have it come so close to our own doors that we almost seem to hear the groaning of the straining timbers and the agonizing shrieks of the doomed men.

And the wreck, any diver will tell you, just has to be out there, not far from shore. Perhaps the secret of her location is already known waiting to be revealed at the right moment, when the lost **Chicora**, after more than a century of waiting and speculation, will be found.

PROPELLER CHICORA.

Built at Detroit in 1892. Foundered during a gale in Lake Michigan, January 21, 1895; all on board perished.

From "*American Steam Vessels*," Copyright 1895, by Smith & Stanton.

CHICORA
Lost on Lake Michigan

SAUGATUCK

MARITIME SERIES

Book 3

By Kit Lane

PAVILION PRESS
P. O. Box 250
Douglas, Michigan 49406

Copyright 1996

By Pavilion Press

All Rights Reserved

Library of Congress Catalog Card Number: 96-67243

International Standard Book Number
1-877703-02-8

Cover: The drawing of the **Chicora** on the cover was done by Walter K. Campbell of the Detroit, Belle Isle and Windsor Ferry Co. for the *Detroit Free Press*. In the background are a few of the hundreds of headlines that the **Chicora** has generated over the last century.

Headlines illustrated at the beginnings of chapters 3 through 8 are from the *Detroit Free Press*.

Back Cover: A detail from a watercolor painting by Royal H. Milleson shows the **Chicora** with steam up on the Chicago River. This would be the view from the Rush Street bridge. The painting is dated 1895. It is on display at the Allegan County Historical Society Museum, Allegan

Table of Contents

1. The Company and the Boat 6
2. One Last Trip 23
3. A Telegram Arrives Too Late: Monday, January 21 31
4. Is No News Good News? Tuesday January 22 35
5. Wreckage at South Haven: Wednesday, January 23 37
6. Out on the Ice Floes: Thursday, January 24 45
7. Quick Look by Yawl: Friday, January 25 51
8. A Committee Takes Action: Saturday, January 26 53
9. A Storm-Forced Interlude: Sunday, January 27 59
10. Masts Found Near Douglas: Monday, January 28 63
11. The **Dickinson** Tries: Tuesday, January 29 67
12. **Petoskey** Freed for the Moment: Wednesday, January 30 70
13. A Brother Is Ready to Sail: Thursday, January 31 73
14. The **Ludington** Searches the Coast: Friday, February 1 75
15. Captain Robertson's Story: Saturday, February 2 77
16. "Is It the **Chicora**?" Sunday, February 3 79
17. The Spark Extinguished: Monday, February 4 90
18. The Search 93
19. Eyewitnesses 98
20. Messages Ashore 106
21. Wreckage 111
22. The Victims 121
23. Tributes and Memorials 135
24. The Search Continues 149
    Index 153
    Illustration Credits 158

1

The Company and the Boat

Lake Michigan was always in the way. When a grower in the northern midwest wanted to send his produce to eastern markets, or to the East Coast for export, the Great Lakes were an obstacle to a direct route. If he chose to use rail the entire distance that meant many extra miles to go around the water and through the busy rail yards of Chicago. But the bottleneck of the big city could be avoided by transporting the goods by rail to Milwaukee where the shipment would be loaded onto steamboats for the cross lake trip, then unloaded at rail terminals in Michigan. Farther north the Ann Arbor railroad ferries and the Pere Marquette railroad ferries accomplished this by carrying already loaded box cars of produce, but Graham & Morton were not railroad ferries, they carried their goods only by contract. However, the railroad contracts were an important part of their business, especially in the wintertime.

In addition to flour the steamers were outfitted to carry other products of Lake Michigan ports: lumber and other wood products from the forests, fruit and vegetables from farmers on both sides of the lake, and passengers needing transportation from port to port to transact business or take a vacation.

The Graham & Morton Transportation Company which was founded in 1875 was essentially the creation of three men: John H. Graham, Andrew Crawford, and J. Stanley Morton. Many of the early records of the company have been lost and the exact legal agreements between the three men, and the original provisions for ownership of various parts of the business, are not described in company archives.

John H. Graham

John Henry Graham was born December 10, 1849, in Boone County, Illinois, the son of John and Lucinda (Nichols) Graham. He spent most of his early years in Elkhart, Indiana, and moved to St. Joseph, Michigan, with his parents in 1864. Later accounts would claim that his first job was driving oxen at $18 a week. His father was engaged in the hardwood lumber business. When John was 17 years old his father became ill and the doctors recommended a change of climate. The elder Graham turned his sawmill over to his teenage son and went West. Later when the father returned to Michigan he found the mill flourishing and a considerable sum of money deposited in his bank account.

After his father's return young Graham branched out on his own, running a sawmill with Andrew Crawford using logs floated down the Paw Paw River to a mill in Benton Harbor. This enterprise led directly to need a for transportation for their lumber products and the founding of the shipping line in 1875. John Graham was also the president of the Alden Canning Company of Benton Harbor, an officer of the St. Joseph Hotel Co. which built a large hotel of that name on the beach at St. Joseph, and was a director of the Union Banking Co. of St. Joseph.

J. H. GRAHAM, President

In 1881 Graham was married to Dora E. Chase of Benton Harbor, formerly of Homer, Michigan. They lived in a large home on Broad Street in St. Joseph. The residence had a tower that overlooked Lake Michigan from the top of the bluff. The couple had no children.

The hotel burned in 1898, but the Graham & Morton Co. was at its peak of prosperity when Graham died, January 9, 1907, from typhoid fever. He was 58 years old.

Andrew Crawford

Andrew Crawford was born in Scotland in 1831 where his father was manager for the Duke-Portland Coal Mines. Young Andrew was educated in Scotland, and later London, and sailed for America in November of 1852. After changing ships in the Azores he arrived in the United States, February 25, 1853, with not one cent in his pocket. According to family tradition he sold his Scottish overcoat in order to gain operating funds. He worked in railroad construction in several U. S. cities including New Orleans and arrived in Illinois in the mid 1850's. He was married in 1857 to Sarah Louise Baxter of Geneseo, Illinois, whose father was a Cape Cod sea captain. Crawford studied law and was admitted to the bar in Illinois in 1860, the same year that he became a naturalized American citizen. He resided in Geneseo and was elected as a Republican to several different political offices. He served four years in the Illinois State Senate, was named as delegate to the Republican national convention in 1872, and was appointed by the governor as a trustee to investigate state institutions.

He moved to Chicago in 1873 and, in 1877, was one of the incorporators, and later vice-president of the Western Indiana Railroad. Crawford had a busy Chicago law practice and became attorney for the street railway interests of the city. He was also on the Board of Commissioners for Lincoln Park which was located not far from his home at 109 Pine Grove. Shortly after moving to Chicago he invested in Michigan lands, and purchased a tract of land on a bluff overlooking Lake Michigan, three and a half miles south of St. Joseph where he built a large summer residence at Royalton Heights. In Michigan he became acquainted with John H. Graham and the two men owned a lumberyard in Benton Harbor which had its own sawmill operation, and docks, both in Michigan and in Chicago.

Andrew Crawford

Crawford's financial interest in Graham & Morton was so considerable that one newspaper said he "owned" the **Chicora**. He has also been described as the company's "financial officer."

When Crawford died in 1900 the company had to purchase his interest in the vessels from the estate, giving the heirs, in partial payment, full ownership of the Chicago dock property. At his death Andrew Crawford had five surviving children: Richard C. of Chicago; Jessie C., the wife of Burdette C. Barnes of Chicago; Daisy C., the wife of T. G. Milsted of New York City; Lucy C., the wife of Frank P. Graves, formerly of Benton Harbor, later a practicing attorney with offices in St. Joseph and Chicago; and Andrew H., who ran the Crawford Transportation Co., which operated passenger and freight boats between Chicago and Saugatuck, 1909 to 1913.

J. Stanley Morton

James Stanley Morton was born September 16, 1850, the son of Henry C. and Josephine (Stanley) Morton of Benton Harbor. His grandfather, Eleazer Morton, was a native of Massachusetts, who moved to Michigan in 1834, and settled in Berrien County, in 1835, being one of the earliest settlers on the eastern shore of Lake Michigan. In the spring of 1836 he built a log tavern on the territorial road near the mouth of the St. Joseph River. He began cultivation of fruit for the Chicago market in 1840, one of the first commercial orchards on the western Great Lakes. Eleazer's son, Henry C. Morton, continued the farm and fruit cultivation and served in the Michigan state legislature in 1863.

At the age of 15 J. Stanley Morton began his business career as clerk in a general store in Benton Harbor. From 1869 to 1873 he was in the drug business in Benton Harbor. He left the retail business altogether in 1874 and chartered the **Lake Breeze** to carry both freight and passengers between Benton Harbor and Chicago. Morton also served as vice president of the First National Bank of Benton Harbor, treasurer of the Alden Canning Co., president of the Stevens & Morton Lumber Co., and secretary of the Benton Harbor Improvement Co.

He was involved in the active leadership of the boat company when it was organized in 1875, but held only two shares in the reorganized company of 1880 although he continued to serve as an officer and on the board of directors. A biography of Morton, published in Charles Moore's *History of Michigan* in 1915, indicates that he was secretary-treasurer of the firm until 1893 when he withdrew, to devote time and investment capital to a number of business ventures including the Excelsior Gas Co., later reorganized as the Benton Harbor and St. Joseph Gas and Fuel Co., a firm he served as vice-president until his withdrawal in 1912; and the Peck Furniture Co. of Benton Harbor of which he was president. In accounts of the 1895 **Chicora** disaster, Morton played an active part in the search for wreckage and bodies, but none of the contemporary accounts gives him a title, or indicates that he acted with any authority other than that given him by Graham who was president of the firm. In 1898 Crawford retired from active administration of the Graham & Morton Co., although he continued to hold a large financial interest, and Morton resumed his role as secretary-treasurer, a position he held until the death of Graham in 1907 when he succeeded to the presidency.

J. Stanley Morton

Morton was later a major stockholder and president of the *Benton Harbor News-Palladium*, which had been formed in 1904 by a merger of the *Evening News* and the *Benton Harbor Palladium*, a newspaper which had been established in 1868.

James Stanley Morton was married in 1871 to Carrie Heath and had four sons. Charles and Henry died young; Raymond, died in 1913, leaving an infant daughter; and William H., who was for years in charge of the Chicago offices of the Graham &

Morton lines. However all of his children preceded him in death. Morton lived to be 87 years old, succumbing October 1, 1936, at his home on Morton Hill in Benton Harbor. He was buried in the Morton Hill Cemetery nearby. By the time of his death the **City of Grand Rapids** was the only vessel owned by the Graham & Morton branch of the Goodrich Line which had already declared bankruptcy. The vessel lay at the Central Dock in Benton Harbor waiting to be sold, but in deference to its fallen leader an old American flag was found and flown at half mast from her main flagstaff.

The Morton family home, 501 Territorial Road, Benton Harbor, was given to the Benton Harbor Women's Club and was later restored and arranged to serve as a museum. It is open to the public from mid-April to the end of October.

Graham & Morton Transportation Co.

In 1874 John Graham and Andrew Crawford were engaged in the sawmill business in Benton Harbor. The waste slabs from the milling process were not marketable and disposal was beginning to pose a problem. Their solution was to start a steamboat business which would not only be used to transport their own products, but would use the slabs as fuel.

The predecessor to the Graham & Morton Transportation Co., called Graham & Morton & Co., was formed in 1875 by John H. Graham, J. S. Morton, Andrew Crawford and James Paxton. The proposal was to start a steamboat line that would link the growers and lumber yards on the St. Joseph River with growing markets in Chicago. Graham became president of the new company and Morton, secretary-treasurer.

There were actually two towns near the mouth of the St. Joseph River. The older of the two, St. Joseph, on the south bank of the river was incorporated as a village in 1834 although it had been the site of a French fort as early as 1679. The second town grew around the tavern of Eleazer Morton between the north bank of the St. Joseph and the Paw Paw river. According to an early history, in 1858 a rickety wooden bridge across the St. Joseph river washed out and when the three leading citizens of the north bank, Eleazer Morton, Sterne Brunson and Charles Hull, went to St. Joseph to ask for assistance with rebuilding of the bridge they were refused. The three then hired a Chicago company to build a canal 25 feet wide from the St. Joseph River into the business district of their settlement. The canal was widened to 50 feet in 1865 and 75 feet in 1875 about the time Graham & Morton & Co. began business. The company maintained extensive docks and warehouses on Water Street in Benton Harbor. Passengers and freight from St. Joseph were usually ferried across the river.

On February 26, 1880, Graham & Morton & Co. was reorganized as the Graham & Morton Transportation Co., a stock company with 500 shares and $50,000 capital. There were only four shareholders, Henry W. Williams, a Benton Harbor saw mill owner, with 197 shares; Andrew Crawford, 151; J. H. Graham, 150; and J. S. Morton, 2. The principal office of the company was at Hinsdale, Du Page County, Illinois. The major contribution to the company by Williams, according to company records, was his interest in the steamer **Skylark**. The company was so structured that Crawford and Graham essentially ran it. Many annual meetings Graham simply sent Crawford a proxy to vote his shares. One or the other was president, and the board of directors, which was named annually, was usually Graham, Crawford and Morton.

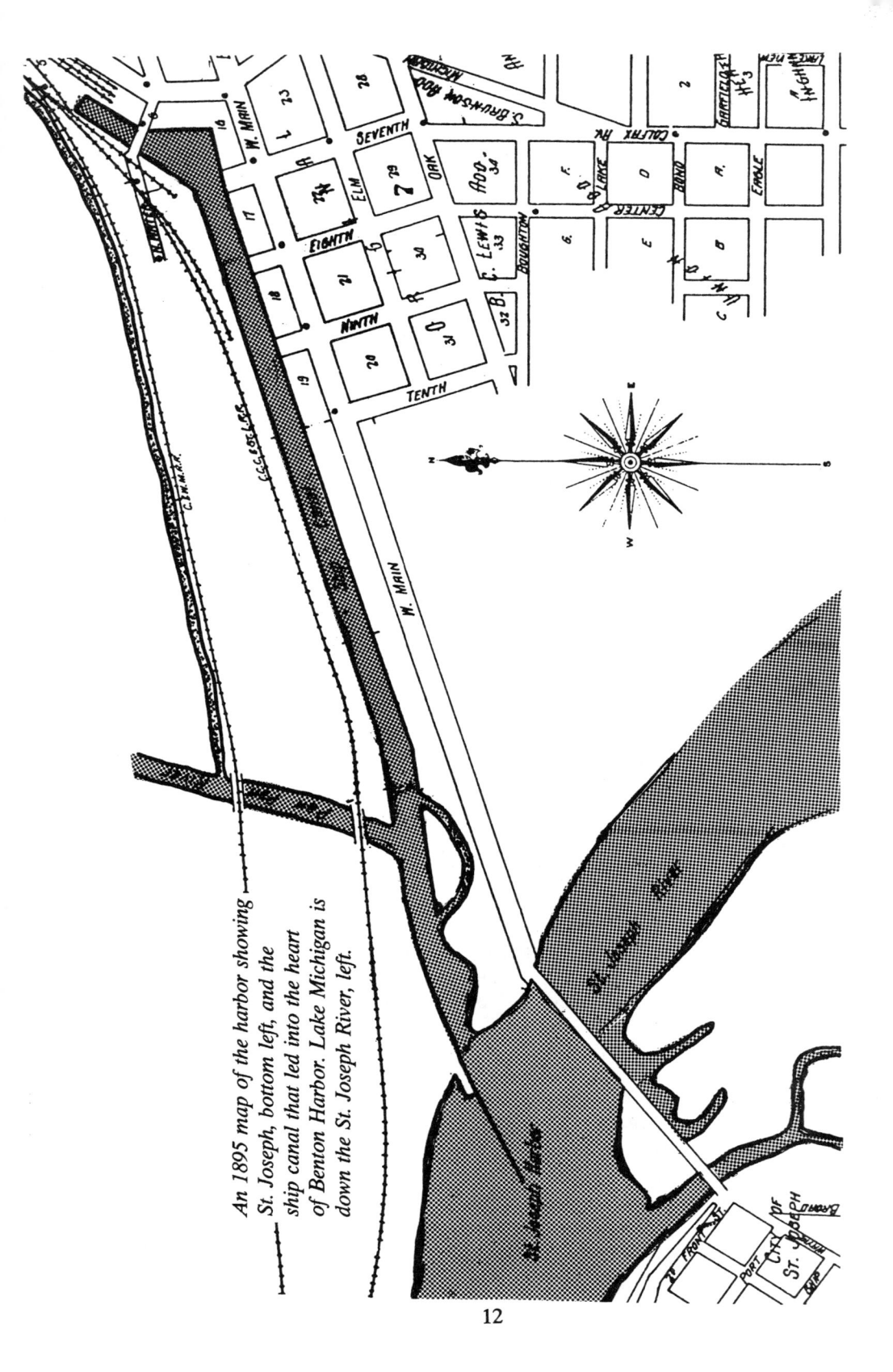

An 1895 map of the harbor showing St. Joseph, bottom left, and the ship canal that led into the heart of Benton Harbor. Lake Michigan is down the St. Joseph River, left.

The company's first act in the reorganization was to purchase from the old company its two active vessels, the **Messenger**, a 444 ton, screw driven steamer 147 feet long, which had been built at Cleveland in 1866, and the **Skylark**, 114 tons, 122 feet in length, which had been built at Detroit in 1864. After a new hull was constructed to receive the old machinery, the **Skylark** was renamed the **Berrien**, after the county in Michigan where St. Joseph and Benton Harbor are located.

In 1882 the fleet was increased by the construction at Benton Harbor of the large propeller **Lora**, named for the daughter of H. W. Williams. The **Lora** was the largest of the boats, listed at 616 tons, 170 feet in length. The following year the **City of St. Joseph**, another propeller, 464 tons, 152 feet long was added, but she was in service for Graham & Morton for only one year. In 1884 the vessel was badly damaged by fire. It was the first loss the line had sustained in over a decade of business.

Following the fire the burned out hulk of the **City of St. Joseph** was purchased by H. W. Williams for the amount of his interest in the Graham & Morton Co. plus $2,857.97. Williams assumed all debt and liens that remained on the vessel and also signed an agreement that he would never compete with Graham & Morton at the twin ports of Benton Harbor and St. Joseph, and that he would never sell the boat to someone who would. Williams then left for South Haven where he founded a line of boats linking that port with Chicago.

In 1887 the **Puritan** was constructed for the Graham & Morton Co. by J. H. Randall at Benton Harbor and put into service. She was screw driven, 290 gross tons, 172 feet in length.

As more steamer lines entered the available markets, the vessels became faster and more luxurious to attract the passenger trade. In 1890 Graham & Morton focused on the passengers with the palatial **City of Chicago** a sidewheeler built at the F. W. Wheeler & Co. yard in West Bay City, Michigan. She was 1,073 tons and 211 feet in length as first constructed, and later lengthened more than 40 feet.

The success of the **City of Chicago** made it clear that the **Puritan** was too small for the task and an order was placed in December of 1891 with the Detroit Drydock Co. for a new vessel. Graham returned to St. Joseph just before New Year's Day, 1892, and announced that the new steamer would be a propeller, over 200 feet in length and "similar to the **Indiana** of the Goodrich line but finished up in a more elaborate style. . . a magnificent steamer in every respect and well adapted to the needs of the route and the demands of the company's business." She would cost $160,000 and would be ready for delivery by the last of May.

Marine architect Frank E. Kirby was responsible for her design and much thought went into both design and material. As the St. Joseph newspaper explained:

> In her building several necessary points have been kept in mind, among them being the necessity of having a boat that could successfully battle with winter's storms and ice and render pleasing service in the summer season in both freight and excursion lines. Wood instead of steel was therefore used as building material and in looking through the boat one is strongly impressed with her great strength and general careful build.

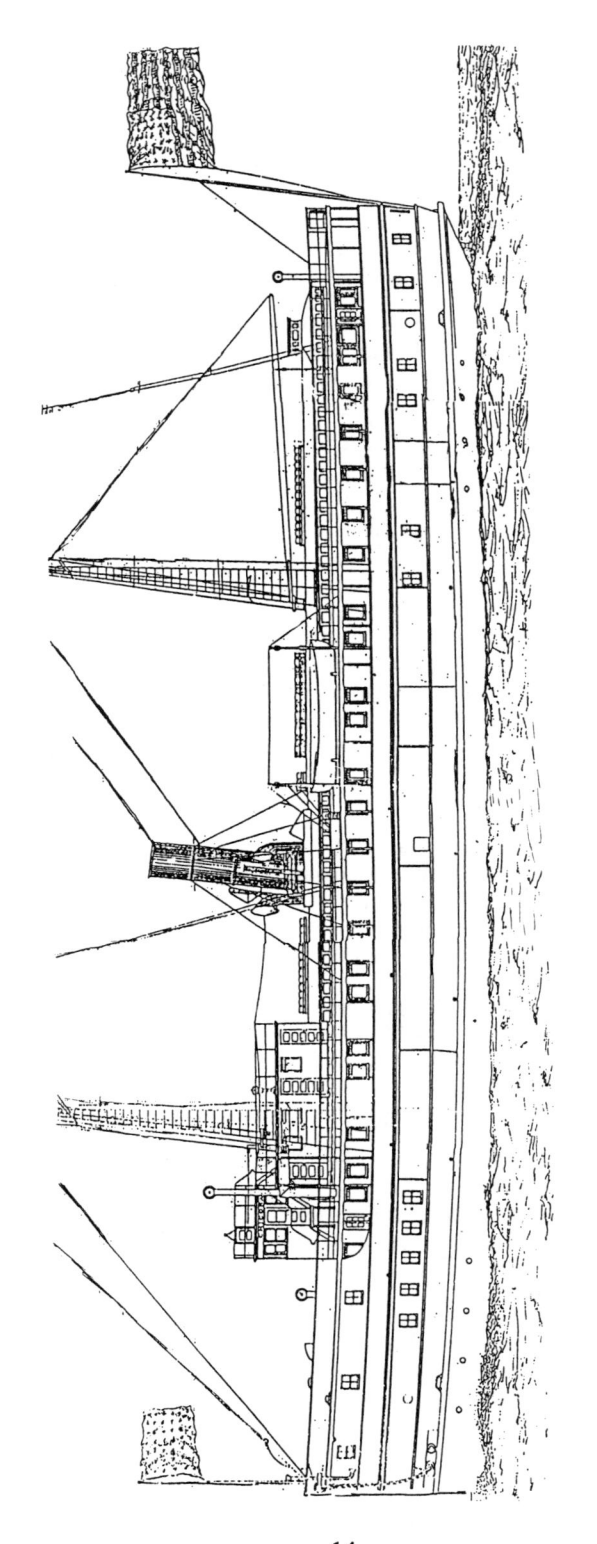

A side view of the Chicora from the plans used during her construction at the Detroit Drydock Co. in 1892.

GRAHAM AND MORTON TRANSPORTATION CO.

ELEGANT NEW STEAMERS

"CITY OF CHICAGO" AND "CHICORA"

Connect with the Chicago & West Michigan, Detroit, Lansing & Northern, Cleveland, Cincinnati, Chicago & St. Louis and Vandalia Ry's for all Northern and Southern Points.

LAKE TICKETS CAN BE SECURED OF YOUR RAILROAD AGENT.

FREIGHT AND PASSENGER RATES LOWER THAN ALL RAIL.

DOCK AND OFFICE, FOOT OF WABASH AVENUE, CHICAGO, ILL.

Advertisement from an 1893 Beeson's Marine Directory

She was launched at Detroit on June 25, 1892, and named at the time of launch. There is nothing in the Detroit newspapers during her building and launch, or in the St. Joseph newspapers at the time of her launch or later on her arrival that would indicate by whom, or why she was named **Chicora**.

An earlier vessel named **Chicora** was a 740 gross ton, 221 foot long steamer built in Birkenhead, England, by William C. Miller & Son in 1864. Very early in her life she was sometimes known as **Let Her B**, a reference to her hull number at the yards which was the letter B. She was first owned by the Chicora Company of Charleston, South Carolina, and used as a blockade runner for the Confederacy during the American Civil War. The boat is credited with taking a large quantity of southern gold to the Caribbean in the closing days of the war. At the end of the war she was sold to northern interests. To get to the Great Lakes the vessel was cut apart to negotiate the Lachine Canal, bypassing rapids on the St. Lawrence river near Montreal, Canada, and reassembled after passage. In 1870 she carried Canadian troops under Viscount Garnet Wolseley to the northwest to put down the Reil Rebellion. Because an international treaty forbids armed foreign troops within the boundaries of the United States, the troops had to disembark on the Canadian side of the St. Mary's river and march around the rapids, reloading upriver. However, tradition maintains that the first load to make the trip were smuggled up the river concealed in the hold of the ship. This is said to be the only instance in history where this law was violated by Canadian forces. In 1878 the **Chicora** became part of the Niagara Navigation Co., Ltd., of Toronto, which operated passenger boats between Queenston, Lewiston and Niagara-on-the-Lake. Most of their vessels had similar names, many of Indian origin, that started with C and ended with A. In addition to the **Chicora**, they ran the **Chippewa, Cibola, Corona, Cayuga** and **Ongiara** (a variant of Niagara). The word Chicora is derived from Shakori, a name given by Spanish explorers in 1521 to Indians then living on the coast of South Carolina. Some authorities have translated it to mean "land of the pretty flowers." The **Chicora** of 1864 was later renamed the **Warrenko** and ran on the Great Lakes until she was rammed and sunk by the **Sprucebay** in Kingston harbor in 1938.

Whatever the reason for the name, it was announced before the launch. The *Detroit Free Press* for June 25, 1892, reported that: "The launch of the **Chicora** will take place at 3 p.m. today at the Orleans street yard."

A story in the June 26 issue of the *Detroit Free Press* describes the day:

Launch of the Chicora

The City Hall clock had scarcely ceased striking 3 yesterday afternoon when the steamer **Chicora** started down the way at the Orleans street yard and in a few seconds time was floating gracefully in the stream several hundred yards from the dock line. A tug soon brought her up to the shears where she will lie until her machinery is hoisted in. A thousand or more people witnessed the launch and a good many others were "just a moment too late."

As the sidewheel steamer **Kirby** is Frank E. Kirby's masterpiece in metal ship-building, so undoubtedly will the **Chicora** prove to be in wood. Her lines are as symmetrical and beautiful as any yacht and with the powerful machinery ready to be placed in her, the boat must be very fast. Her engine is triple expansion, cylinders 21,33 and 52 by 42 inch stroke. She will have two steel boilers, 12 feet in diameter and 12 feet long, constructed for a pressure of 165 pounds. Howden's forced draft attachment will be provided. The **Chicora's** dimensions are: Length over all, 210 feet; keel, 197 feet; breadth, 35 feet; extreme breadth, 39 1/2 feet. She will have a 250-light electric light plant, and in general finish she will be similar to the **Indiana**.

She will have fifty-six state rooms, large smoking room and a spacious social hall. The cabins as well as the grand staircase and gangway between the decks, will all be finished in mahogany. She will have sleeping room for 200 passengers and an excursion license for 1,500. She will be schooner-rigged, with standing gaffs and booms. The boilers and machinery will be placed exactly in the center of the boat.

At her launch the exterior looked finished, but interior decoration was yet to be completed and the boilers and the machinery were not yet installed. Graham & Morton officials would have liked to hurry the fitting out of the new vessel. The newly-formed St. Joseph & Lake Michigan Transportation Co. had started passenger and freight service from St. Joseph to both Chicago and Milwaukee in May of 1892, using the **Soo City** and the **Lora** which had originally been a G & M vessel. It was hoped that the **Chicora** might win back some of the customers lost to the new line.

*The **Chicora** entering St. Joseph harbor in 1893*

However, it was after several delays that she actually entered the mouth of the St Joseph River for the first time on Monday, August 15. The August 20, 1892, issue of the *St. Joseph Saturday Herald* described the scene:

Arrival of the Chicora

The long-looked for new steamer **Chicora**, of the G. & M. line, came into port Monday morning, about 6 o'clock and was given a most royal welcome in the shape of the usual salute of whistles from tugs and factories. A few early risers only, however, were out to see and greet her but people soon left tables and work to go and look the new craft over. She had been in mind so many weeks, so much talked over, so much looked forward to as something that would surely be worthy of a kindly welcome and appreciation that everybody felt she must be seen and inspected at the earliest opportunity after her arrival, hence from early morning until after night the new boat passed under many critical eyes and there was only one voice following -- "she is all right."

The President of the Company, Mr. J. H. Graham, was one of the first to greet her and he with other officers took pardonable pride in showing the product of their season's time, money and labor. The **Chicora** left Detroit at 12:10 Saturday morning in charge of Capt. Levi Mann, made several stops on the way, amounting in all to about 11 hours, reaching here at the hour named above, thus making the distance in 43 hours. Everything worked nicely and the expectations of the owners were quite realized in her initial trip.

Captain Edward Stines, who would be her captain, Steward Charles Springsteen and others who would be part of her regular crew took the train to Detroit and rode back around the lakes. Joining them were Mrs. E. A. Graham (sister-in-law of J. H. Graham) and her daughter May, Mr. and Mrs. John F. Gard, Mr. and Mrs. Joseph F. Pearl, Mrs. Dempster, Miss Margaret Kingsland, and Miss Bartram from St. Joseph; Mr. and Mrs. Monroe Morrow and daughter, Miss Alta Conger, J. S. Morton and two sons, Mr. and Mrs. Charles Bowman and son, and Fred Hopkins of Benton Harbor; and Captain and Mrs. George H. Simpson of Cleveland and C. B. Palmer and Will Snyder of Detroit.

"She is elegantly finished and furnished and arranged in every part with an eye to business, convenience and comfort," the newspaper explained. "To appreciate the boat more fully one must personally inspect the details of her construction and equipment. Like the other steamers of this route she is lighted with numerous incandescent lights, with colored shades, and these help in the general rich and pleasing effects of her beautiful cabin." Archer the florist sent an elegant floral basket with an attached card which read, "The Chicora -- the Flagship of the East Shore."

Her first crew included, in addition to Captain Stines, first mate, William Russell; second mate, George E. Leggett; first engineer, Robert McClure; purser, William J. Hancock and steward, Charles Springsteen.

Shortly after her arrival at St. Joseph she was sent into Chicago for some additional outfitting and reached the city in three hours and forty-seven minutes, pier to pier. At Chicago she was welcomed by large crowds. After her public inspection **Chicora** took her place in the regular Graham & Morton schedule replacing the **Puritan** which was sold to Seymour Transportation Co. of Chicago. In the summer the **Chicora** usually ran from Benton Harbor to Chicago forming a daily service with the **City of Chicago**. In the fall and sometimes winter, she took mostly freight trips to Milwaukee in connection with the Big Four and Vandalia railroads.

As originally built, with decorating additions added over the next three years, the passenger accommodations of the **Chicora** were, as the St. Joseph newspaper said, "luxuriously furnished":

> The staterooms were finished in the same style as the latest Pullman cars, in mahogany and Lincrusta-Walton. The dining room was finished in mahogany, with tables, chairs and sideboard in oak. The gangway and main staircase were artistic, and the main cabin arched and 100 feet long. She was lighted throughout with electric lights.

Certificate No.	Art. 40, Customs Regs., 1892.	OFFICIAL NUMBER
14		126902

THE UNITED STATES OF AMERICA.

Sec. 4319, Rev. Stats.   Catalogue No. 538½.

Permanent CERTIFICATE OF ENROLLMENT.

(NORTHERN, NORTHEASTERN, AND NORTHWESTERN FRONTIERS OF THE UNITED STATES.)

ENROLLMENT. In conformity to Title L, "REGULATION OF VESSELS IN DOMESTIC COMMERCE," of the Revised Statutes of the United States.

J. H. Graham of St Joseph Michigan having taken and subscribed the oath required by law, and having sworn that he Vice President of the Graham and Morton Transportation Company incorporated under the laws of the State of Illinois, and that said Company are

ship or vessel called the Chicora, of St Joseph, whereof Edward Stines is at present Master, and is a citizen of the United States, and that the said ship or vessel was built at Detroit Michigan in the year 1892, as appears by Temp Enrollment No 16 dated Detroit August 11th 1892, now surrendered arrival Home and said Enrollment having certified that the said ship or vessel has One deck and Two masts, and that her register length is 198 4/10 feet, her register breadth, 35 feet, her register depth, 13 4/10 feet, her height, 10 feet, that she measures 1122 and 92 tons, viz:

	TONS.	100ths.
Capacity under tonnage deck	633	94
Capacity between decks above tonnage deck		
Capacity of inclosures on the upper deck, viz:	488	98
Gross Tonnage	1122	92
*Deductions under Section 4153, Revised Statutes, as amended by Act of March 2, 1895:		
Crew space,.........; Master's cabin,.........;		
Steering gear,.........; Anchor gear,.........;		
Boatswain's stores,.........; Chart house,.........; Storage of sails,.........;		
Donkey engine and boiler,.........; Propelling power,.........;		
Total Deductions	414	77
Net Tonnage	708	15

that the following described spaces, and no others, have been omitted, viz:

and that she is a § Propeller, has a plain head and a round stern, and according to the said Title, the said SHIP or VESSEL has been duly ENROLLED at the Port of Grand Haven, Given under my hand and seal at the Port of Grand Haven, in the District of Michigan, this 19th day of August, in the year one thousand eight hundred and ninety-Two

Saml D Earns
Dep. Collector of Customs.

Naval Officer.

Chicora's first and only permanent enrollment

Graham & Morton Transportation Co's

LINE OF STEAMERS TO CHICAGO AND MILWAUKEE.

The Favorite Passenger Steamers CITY OF CHICAGO and CHICORA will make Double Daily trips between Benton Harbor, St. Joseph and Chicago. The following schedule will be observed on and after June 10th:

CHICAGO DIVISION—Leave Benton Harbor at 2:15 p. m., daily, except Sunday, and at 8:30 p. m., daily, including Sunday. Leave St. Joseph at 4 p. m., daily except Sunday, and at 10 p. m., daily, including Sunday, and Sunday at 6 p. m., also. Leave Chicago at 9:30 a. m. and 11:30 p. m., daily, including Sunday, and Saturdays only at 2 p. m.

MILWAUKEE DIVISION—The Steamer R. C. REID will make tri-weekly trips between Benton Harbor, St. Joseph and Milwaukee, leaving Benton Harbor at 7:30 and St. Joseph at 9 p. m., Mondays, Wednesdays and Fridays. Leave Milwaukee Tuesdays, Thursdays and Saturdays at 7 p. m.

DOCKS—Benton Harbor, J. H. Graham & Co.; St. Joseph, E. A. Graham; Chicago, J. H. Graham & Co., 46 and 48 River street, foot of Wabash avenue; Milwaukee, foot of Broadway.   J. H. GRAHAM, President.

A St. Joseph newspaper advertisement from the summer of 1894

In November of 1893 the **Chicora** was placed in dry dock and, according to company records "ironed for winter service." Portions of the exterior of the hull received an iron sheathing to protect it from ice damage. After her disappearance owner Graham issued a statement in regard to her construction to answer those who were calling the vessel ill-equipped for winter travel:

> When she was built she was built to run expressly between St. Joseph and Milwaukee in the winter service and when this company decided to build such a vessel they applied to Frank E. Kirby of the Detroit Drydock Co.'s works, to draw the design and superintend the construction of a boat adapted to carry 800 tons and run fifteen miles an hour. The company wished, if possible, to build such a vessel of steel, not wishing to invest money in a wooden vessel, but Mr. Kirby, in his judgment, thought only a wooden vessel suitable for it, and he

designed her expressly for it with every convenience for handling her. With that amount of freight she had the most freeboard of any vessel running in the winter trade across Lake Michigan, something like four feet at the lowest point amidships. She was built for handling grain and had grain hatches designed by Mr. Kirby and also for handling freight; in her hold and on deck. Her gangways were not as wide as a good many, and she had two gangways where vessels of her size and length would usually have four. The **Chicora** rated A1 with a star, the highest classification there is. She also had more power than any merchant vessel on the western lakes and her machinery was in first-class condition.

To add to the popularity of the boat, Ben King, a poet from St. Joseph who was gaining national recognition, penned a poem about a trip that he apparently took one day from St. Joseph, the kind of Sunday afternoon excursion that was not bound for anywhere in particular but designed to give local people and tourists an outing of two or three hours on Lake Michigan. Excursions were a source of extra income when there was little freight to load and the next scheduled sailing was not until the following day. The poem was published in 1894, just before the boat was lost. King was perhaps better known as a performer than a writer and presented his own work frequently on the stage. This poem would have been familiar to citizens of the twin cities. The title of the poem, "I Fed the Fishes," is actually a Nineteenth Century euphemism for being seasick. It was a multi-verse narrative, in the fashion of the day.

I FED THE FISHES

One day a big excursion sailed afar out in the lake,
All bent upon an outing with their sandwiches and cake,
They sought the upper deck until the wind began to blow,
When all engaged in different things as every one must know;
    While I fed the fishes,
    I fed the fishes,
I fed the fishes clear to Old St. Joe.

Good Captain Stines went up on deck to cast his weather eye;
A woman sadly, badly prayed, "O Father, let me die!"
The cabin-boys ran back and forth in staterooms all around,
While voices shrieked, "Oh, mercy--oop! Oh--oop wish I were drowned.
    But I fed the fishes,
    I gave them my best wishes,
I fed the fishes clear to Old St. Joe.

The pilot boldly held the wheel as through the waves we sped,
While Purser Hancock ran abaft to hold some woman's head;
One fellow sat him down and sang: "Good-bye, sweetheart, good-bye;"
Most every seemed occupied, and, sad to say, then I --

> I fed the fishes,
> I fed the fishes,
> I fed the fishes clear to Old St. Joe.
>
> The "**Chicora**" rose up in the air and then came down "kersock;"
> She wibble-wobbled in the sea and once she struck a rock;
> The purser wore a pallid look, the women all turned pale,
> While calmly I sat out on deck and hung over the rail;
> > For I fed the fishes,
> > I gave them my best wishes,
> I fed the fishes clear to Old St. Joe.
>
> Some tried to eat their sandwiches, some staggered, reeled and laughed,
> While others went below to smile, and there the brown ale quaffed.
> The steward, Richard Waters, rushed about with whisky slings;
> Most every one seemed occupied, and all did different things,
> > But I fed the fishes,
> > I fed the fishes,
> I fed the fishes clear to Old St. Joe.

All of the above seemed to give the people of St. Joseph and Benton Harbor a special affection for the vessel. Memorial services following the foundering were as much a memorial for the boat itself, as for the lost crewmen.

*A group of visitors pose as the **Chicora** enters St. Joseph. The giant slide is at right.*

2

One Last Trip

Graham & Morton tried to keep winter navigation open as long as ice conditions allowed. Some winters they succeeded in running year round, some seasons they took a few weeks off, or a month, but the plan was to run as often as they had cargo to pay the way.

However, winter needs were usually smaller and, even though the **Chicora** was strongly constructed to navigate the ice, in the winter of 1894-95 they had leased the **Petoskey** from the Northern Michigan Transportation Co., owned principally by the Seymour brothers of Manistee, and planned to lay up the larger boats leaving the **Petoskey** alone on the St. Joseph to Milwaukee run.

The November 24, 1894, issue of the *St. Joseph Saturday Herald*, noted: "The **Chicora** will make her last trip to Chicago on Friday night next." The following week, December 1, the newspaper reported, "Regular navigation between here and Chicago closes today for the winter." The newspaper added that the St. Joseph Life Saving crew was scheduled to go off duty on December 5.

The **Petoskey** was delivered to the Graham & Morton Co. in Milwaukee and went immediately into drydock for repairs and to be specially outfitted for winter service. She arrived in Benton Harbor at 8 a.m. December 12 on her first trip, carrying 37 cars of flour and four cars of barley for transfer to the Big Four railroad and some freight for the Vandalia line. The *Benton Harbor Daily Palladium* described her as "a propeller built somewhat on the model of the **Lora**, but has a much more powerful engine and a carrying capacity of over 700 tons."

The "Big Four," more properly called the Cleveland, Cincinnati, Chicago and St. Louis Railway shipped freight to all of the cities in its name, and had connections to overseas cargo ships. The Vandalia Railroad primarily served Indiana with terminals in Indianapolis, Peoria and Terre Haute, Indiana, and St. Louis, Missouri, and headquarters at Terre Haute, Indiana.

The Graham & Morton company was trying to get the **R. C. Reid** into drydock to be lengthened over the winter, but the vessel made at least one more trip. An item in the December 22 *St. Joseph Saturday Herald* reported: "The three G & M steamers brought in large cargoes of freight from Milwaukee, for the Big Four this week." The **City of Chicago** was never considered a winter boat. This would leave the **Chicora, Reid** and the chartered ship, the **Petoskey**, to be the three steamers that made at least one trip the week of December 22.

The **Chicora** was taken out of commission for the winter on January 1. Most of her furniture, carpets, piano, and other items, primarily in the passenger cabins and lounges, was taken ashore to be stored for the winter, and work began immediately to place her "in perfect repair."

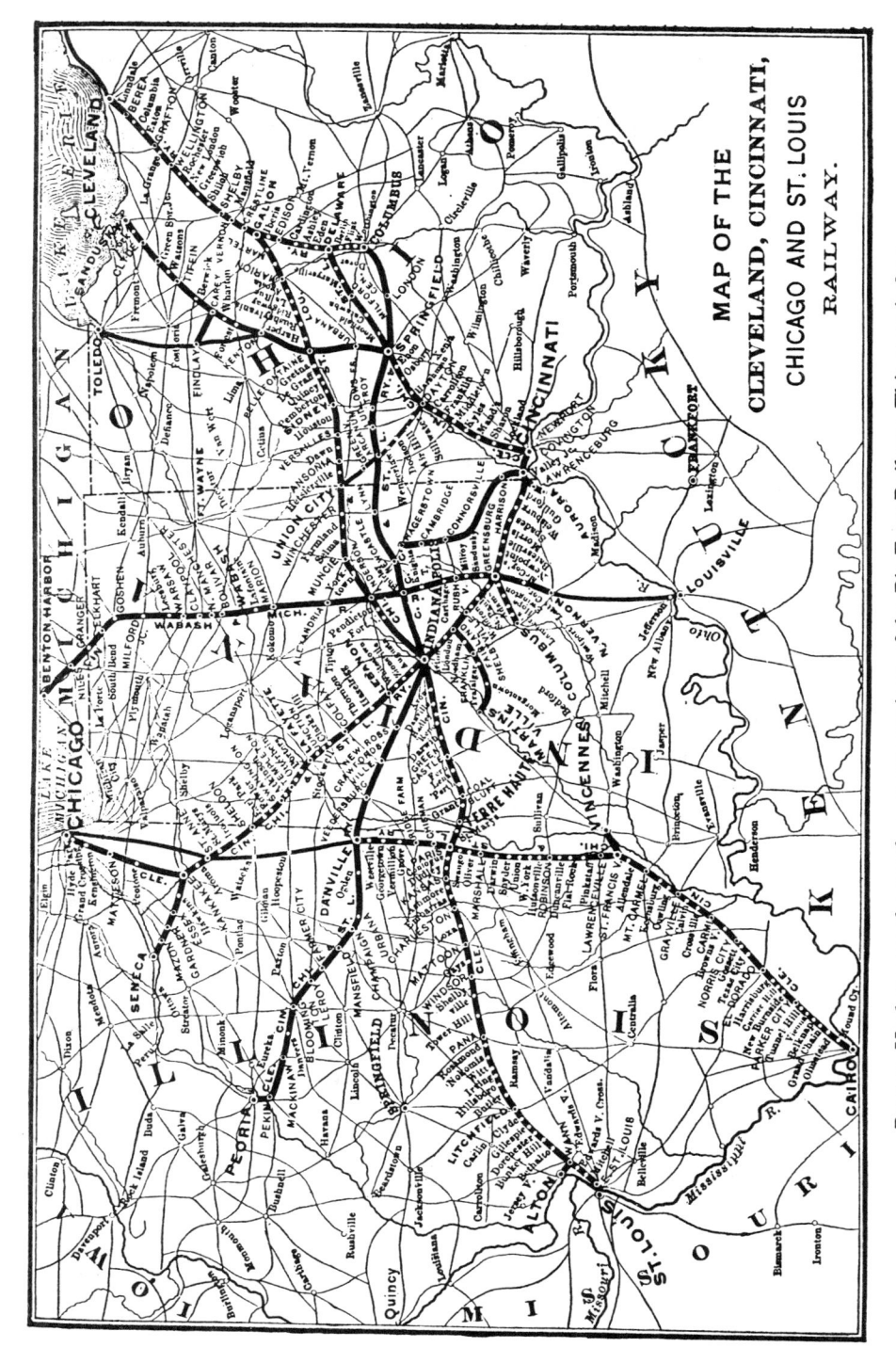

Benton Harbor was the northernmost terminus of the Big Four Railway. This map is from an 1891 Poor's Manual of Railroads.

But there were unusual demands for freight service in the fall and winter of 1895-96. Because of cool, wet weather there was a particularly late harvest of wheat in the upper midwest. Into January the flour mills were still operating and barrels and bags of flour were piling up in Milwaukee warehouses. The flour was coming in faster than a boat the size of the **Petoskey** could handle alone. On the Michigan side of the lake the buildup of ice and bad weather was creating delays in shipping for even the stalwart **Petoskey**.

The railroads were demanding better service. They were often frustrated in the winter when the weather caused delays for boat traffic. When this happened notices would begin appearing in the newspapers that the Big Four railway, one of G & M's biggest customers, was looking into alternate routes that would eliminate the cross-lake traffic and make the entire trip by rail, or leave from a port less susceptible to ice blockades than Benton Harbor. The January 17, 1895, *Detroit Tribune*, fueled the speculation: "It is rumored here today dissatisfactions and refusal of right of ways at St. Joseph have caused the Big Four railway to seek another seaport terminus. Their steamers are stuck in the ice more or less, and they will shortly extend the line to this city [Detroit], where they can have their navigation uninterrupted." Another newspaper story mentioned crossing the lake to Muskegon and then traveling south by rail.

Since their contract with the Big Four Railway was an important part of their annual income, the Graham & Morton officials felt it important to put forth the extra effort needed to retain the business. To this end a decision was made to reoutfit the **Chicora** for a least one more freight run to Milwaukee.

Her owners were aware that the boat would have to sail without insurance on either vessel or cargo. Some accounts claim that the **Chicora** was considered so seaworthy that marine insurance was never carried, but, being a wooden boat during the regular season she sailed with fire insurance valuing the vessel at $100,000; $140,000 including the furnishings. However, most companies that insured Lakes vessels would not provide coverage during the winter, and it was long past the cutoff date.

As men hurried to prepare the **Chicora**, ice began to form along the coast. On Monday, January 14, the **Petoskey** started to Milwaukee with a small cargo and one passenger, Alderman M. H. Morrow of Benton Harbor. At the end of the south pier she got caught in a large ice field and was immobilized. The fishing tug **Tramp** tried all day Wednesday and part of Thursday to free her. Her discouraged passenger walked ashore just as the wind shifted and the ice parted from the shore and floated out into the lake carrying the imprisoned steamer with it. The larger tug **T. T. Morford** was sent for from Chicago, and for a while the **Petoskey,** the fishing tug **Tramp** and the towing tug **Morford** were all stuck in an ice floe which was drifting down the lake with northwesterly winds. Finally Friday afternoon, January 18, the steamer was released and continued on to Milwaukee. The **Morford**, which had damaged a rudder in the operation, put into St. Joseph for repairs.

The stockpiles of flour awaiting shipment continued to grow in Milwaukee. The same *Benton Harbor Daily Palladium* newspaper, dated Saturday, January 19, that described the release of the **Petoskey** noted:

> The steamer **Chicora** which has been moored at the G & M
> dock here for a couple of weeks, plowed her way through the ice in

the canal this forenoon and is now taking on a load of freight at the Vandalia warehouse preparatory to clearing for Milwaukee this evening. The ice in the canal is about 10 inches in thickness and the steamer was enabled to break her way through without difficulty.

As the steamer loaded a crew was gathering. The chief engineer, Robert McClure, had been wired at his home in Detroit and arrived by train. Before long McClure, second engineer Alfred Wirtz, James E. Malone, Grant and Ralph Downing, John Werner and William Miller had arrived at the Gartley House in Benton Harbor, an establishment practically adjacent to the G & M docks, where they boarded when not on the vessel. The landlord at the Gartley House, a man named Wilcox, said later that the Friday before the boat left "some of the men were skating on the ice back of the house while others were playing pedro and Mr. McClure was rehearsing some of his war stories with Captain Griffin [captain of the **Petoskey**]. The next morning they were notified that the boat was steaming up preparatory to leaving for Milwaukee. It makes me heartsick which I think back and see those men standing on the deck of the **Chicora** while she was breaking her way out of the harbor for the last time."

William J. Hancock, regular clerk of the **Chicora**, was in Saugatuck visiting his wife, Caddie, who had been ill. To get to Benton Harbor from Saugatuck required a carriage ride nine miles north to Holland or six miles west to New Richmond, where he could catch the Chicago and West Michigan Railway train. Or if the shoreline allowed navigation, a fishing tug might have carried him north to the Holland train station. Some accounts record that he had "misunderstood the time of sailing" and did not arrive in Benton Harbor in time. The *Three Oaks Press* described the circumstances that put James R. Clarke, who sailed as clerk, and passenger Joseph F. Pearl aboard:

> James R. Clarke and Druggist Pearl of St. Joseph lost their lives and William J. Hancock saved his through merest chance. For 10 days the **Chicora** has been laid up in Benton Harbor and Hancock had gone to Saugatuck to visit his bride of a few months. He failed to get the train which reached St. Joseph before it was time for the steamer to sail. President Graham found James R. Clarke, who had formerly served the line as clerk on its steamers, in Mr. Pearl's drug store. "Jim, Hancock isn't here; you must go over on the **Chicora** tonight," Mr. Graham said to Mr. Clarke. "All right; I'll go if Joe will go with me." Mr. Pearl agreed, and in half an hour the two were on the way to the steamer.

According to a later statement by Grosvenor Tarbell of Milwaukee, Doc Ballenger, an overall manufacturer in St. Joseph, was also asked to join the expedition and at first accepted, but later decided not to go. Tarbell was also invited to return to his home on the **Chicora** but declined because he had not yet completed his business in Michigan. These circumstances led to early reports from Milwaukee that the captain had four guests aboard the boat.

The weather was unseasonably moderate. A diary kept by Charles Decker of Bangor, a regular crew member who missed the last sailing because of illness recorded that on Saturday it was "balmy and springlike."

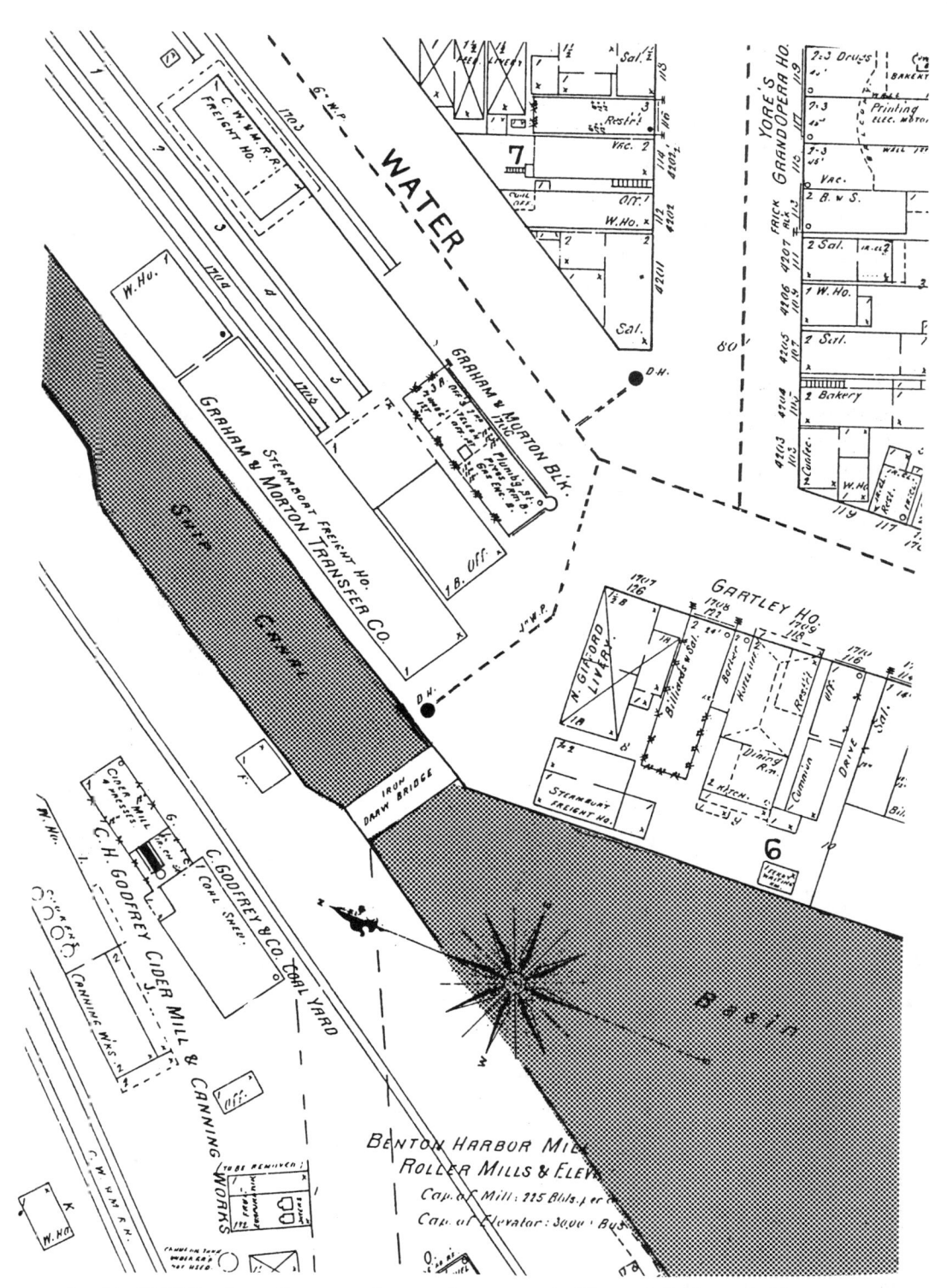

In this 1895 Sanborn fire map, the warehouses and offices of Graham & Morton and nearby telegraph office are shown at the end of the canal, upper left, near the rail lines.

Boat traffic at the port on the St. Joseph was busy. The Monday, January 21 issue of the *Benton Harbor Daily Palladium* carried the terse column:

The Boats

The **Petoskey** arrived from Milwaukee Sunday morning.

The tug **T. T. Morford** cleared for Chicago Sunday morning.

The steamer **Chicora** cleared for Milwaukee Sunday morning.

According to one account the **Chicora** left shortly after the **Petoskey** arrived making use of the path that the returning boat had cut through the ice field. Even with that assistance it was more than an hour after she left the dock that the vessel broke into open water.

The **Chicora** arrived at Milwaukee about 5 p.m. on Sunday. An incident that occurred just before entering the harbor would later be discussed at length as an omen. The most complete account was given in the *Milwaukee Sentinel* for January 24:

> Joseph Pearl, the only passenger on board of the boat had taken with him a small rifle and a box of cartridges. When six miles off the shore a wild duck was seen flying toward the **Chicora**. Everybody on board of the vessel marveled at the incident, because the sailors never before knew ducks to fly toward a vessel on the sea. Pearl had its rifle handy and when the duck was about to light on the vessel he fired and killed the fowl. He remarked that he was a good marksman and spoke of the matter to Capt. Stines, whose guest he was.
>
> While he was telling the story to the master of the boat, the latter began to turn pale. Pearl asked him what had happened and he remarked:
>
> "My God, Pearl, what have you done? I feel like kneeling down and praying."
>
> He then told the druggist that a duck was never known to fly toward a steamer and that the fact that this one had done so, and that Pearl had killed it was a bad omen. Pearl tried to laugh off the matter, but the master and the crew became downcast from that time on, and they were in a moody state when the boat left this port.

The story about the duck twisted and grew. In the January 31 issue of the *Michigan City Dispatch* the bird had become an "immense gull." The newspaper discussed its importance under the heading:

A SUPERSTITION

> There is a superstition among sailors that "ill-luck follows him who kills a seagull."

A group of sailors were yesterday discussing the loss of the **Chicora** and a story connecting one of the men on board the ill-fated steamer with the killing of a seagull points with unusual force to the belief referred to. The regular clerk of the **Chicora** not being at hand to sail with the steamer Mr. Clark was impressed to take his place, and Druggist Pearl was invited to go also. The latter took with him a rifle and on the way over shot and killed an immense gull. This act had a depressing effect on all on board and it is stated the effect was such on many of the crew that just before the steamer left Milwaukee for the return trip that they talked strongly of refusing to go if the druggist was on board. However, they were persuaded and none are left to tell the history of their awful trials, suffering and death.

Capt. Cochrane, of the steamer **John A. Dix**, on one of his excursion trips to this city two years ago soundly thrashed a frisky excursionist for killing a gull from the deck of the steamer with a revolver. The vessel man who related this incident to the writer also added that he would have done the same thing.

The superstition concerning killing a bird, most commonly a gull or on the open ocean an albatross or petrel, is very old. It was popularized by "The Rime of the Ancient Mariner" written by Samuel T. Coleridge in 1798. In the distant past it was linked to the idea that drowned men were reincarnated as seabirds and that killing one was tantamount to killing a shipmate and evil luck would surely follow.

*The **Chicora** struggles in the ice at the mouth of St. Joseph harbor in December, 1893.*

The hours between 5 p.m. when she arrived and 5:15 a.m. when she would depart, were spent loading a near-capacity cargo of flour and other freight. According to an account in the *Milwaukee Sentinel* of January 25 the cargo was shipped mostly from Minneapolis mills and consigned to Eastern ports for the export trade. It had been brought to Milwaukee from the Chicago, Milwaukee & St. Paul and the Wisconsin Central railroads to be transferred to the Big Four and Vandalia lines. The report itemized the freight:

> The Big Four line's freight was from the following mills: Washburn-Crosby Milling company, Minneapolis, ten cars of flour; T. C. Estee, Minneapolis, ten cars; M H. Sheffield, Mankato, three cars; Peterson Bros., Chicago, one car; Northwestern Consolidated Milling company, Minneapolis, three cars; Listmann Milling company, LaCrosse, one car; Blodgett Milling company, Beloit, one car. The total shipment of the Big Four was twenty-nine cars. The Vandalia line had the following freight: Washburn-Crosby Milling company, Minneapolis, two cars of flour; Mann Bros., Milwaukee, twenty-seven bundles of chairs; Sterns Milling company, Milwaukee, 1,000 sacks of flour; B. Kern & Sons, Milwaukee, two cars of flour; Milwaukee Malt & Grain company, 440 bags of malt.

The whole cargo weighed 632 tons. Although the amount of flour was sometimes expressed in car loads, the **Chicora** carried it in barrels, boxes and bags, and was not equipped to carry loaded railroad cars like some of the car ferries that plied Lake Michigan farther north.

Clerk James Clarke would have been busy overseeing the loading, but Pearl met a number of Milwaukee friends and went to the Davidson theater where they witnessed a performance of "A Temperance Town." Captain Stines, his son and several other officers of the crew were invited to join the party but, according to a *Milwaukee Sentinel* report, "they refused to do so because they said they were not feeling like taking in a show." After the play the theater party returned to the steamer about 2 a.m. to visit the captain. "Pearl and his friends were jovial, but Capt. Stines was downcast and asked them not to be so loud because they would wake the colored porter in the next room. Before the party left the boat that night Stines told a local stockholder that he wished he had resigned his commission last fall and not gone out on the **Chicora**," the *Sentinel* reported. One of the visitors was E. S. Whistler, who was Chicago agent of G & M during the summer and worked at the Milwaukee office during the winter. He later told a reporter that he found the master of the **Chicora** "in a moody condition" and that when they left the captain retired.

3

A Telegram Arrives Too Late

Monday, January 21

By 5 a.m., Milwaukee time, on Monday morning the **Chicora** was loaded and ready to leave. At 5:15 she hoisted anchor and moved slowly out of Milwaukee harbor in a drizzling rain. The lighthouse keeper was the last person who saw the boat.

On the Michigan shore J. H. Graham did not sleep well Sunday night. He awoke very early Monday morning and looked at his barometer. It stood at 28, the lowest he had ever seen. Graham went immediately to the docks to tell the captain of the **Petoskey** not to leave for Milwaukee, and began efforts to find a wire operator to send a message to the **Chicora** to remain in Wisconsin.

Edward Barry, the night telegraph operator at Benton Harbor, was located and sent the message to Milwaukee. Later fanciful accounts would relate how the messenger boy on his bicycle rushed down to the docks just in time to see the big steamer pulling away, or, sometimes, just vanishing over the horizon. No contemporary accounts could be found that corroborate these details. None of the Milwaukee newspapers mention the telegram at all. Operator Barry would later say it missed the departing boat by three minutes. There was some delay in receiving a return message from Milwaukee, but by 10 a.m. the officials in Benton Harbor were aware that the message that would have told the captain not to sail had missed the boat and that the **Chicora** was somewhere out on Lake Michigan.

According to a later story in a Chicago newspaper, which tried to recreate the weather that day, when the **Chicora** left Milwaukee for St. Joseph the wind was blowing 26 miles an hour from the southeast, about half a gale, and there was nothing threatening in the atmospheric conditions. The temperature was 50 and the barometric conditions normal. "Nothing indicated to the man wisest in the weather that it would be more unsafe to sail the lakes on that day than on any other day when navigation is normally closed."

At 9 a.m. (10 Michigan time) the wind began to freshen and a few minutes later storm signals were hoisted at Chicago, where the weather station was located. A wire was also sent to Milwaukee, Grand Haven, Ludington, and Manistee. According to the *Chicago Tribune*, the warning read:

IN DANGER !

THREE BOATS NOW OUT IN THE TERRIBLE STORM.

GREAT ANXIETY EXPRESSED OVER THE STEAMER CHICORA.

THAT BOAT SOMEWHERE ON LAKE MICHIGAN,

WHERE THE WORST STORM FOR YEARS IS NOW RAGING.

FISH TUG TRAMP LYING IN A DANGEROUS POSITION.

SEVERE STORM, CENTRAL AT MILWAUKEE, WITH BAROMETER NEARLY ONE INCH BELOW NORMAL; MOVING TO THE NORTHEAST; WILL SHIFT TO NORTHWEST THIS AFTERNOON; WILL BE DANGEROUS TO ALL SHIPPING.

The brisk breeze continued to increase and the thermometer dropped rapidly. At 10 o'clock (11 Michigan time), after a single hour, the wind was blowing sixty miles an hour, veering to the southwest, and it was 30 degrees above zero. Snow was falling.

By noon the wind included gusts of up to 64 miles an hour and the thermometer stood at 28 degrees. This was the height of the storm which gradually decreased in intensity until by 5 p.m. the winds were just 30 miles an hour, dying out in the west and shifting slowly to the northwest. Oldtimers said that except for the hurricane of February 24, 1894, no such wind has been felt in the area since 1880.

One man in Three Oaks, south and east of St. Joseph, recorded that at 9 a.m. Monday morning the air temperature was a balmy 51 degrees with a thunderstorm raging, rolling thunder and a lot of lightning. As the thunderstorm passed the temperature began to drop dramatically. By 11 a.m. it had fallen 23 degrees and stood at 28 degrees. By 3 p.m. a terrific blizzard was underway.

The **Chicora** was due into St. Joseph by 12:30. When the storm hit it was obvious that the vessel, which would have encountered the dramatic change in weather sometime about mid lake, would be delayed. As hurricane velocity winds blew floating ice against the shore, there was the added worry that even if she got to the mouth of the harbor at St. Joseph, the ice fields would prevent her from entering.

The next day's *Detroit Free Press* reported under a January 21, dateline:

> At 9:30 tonight parties went out on the piers at St. Joseph to sight the **Chicora**, reported fast in the ice a couple of miles off shore. The wind was still blowing at a fearful force with the air full of fine blinding snow; making it almost impossible to see much beyond the lighthouse on the north pier, but between the storm gusts glimpses of a flickering red light, moving up and down as with the rolling sea could be seen plainly, but no distress signals could be seen or heard. As near as can be estimated the boat with the red light was fully five miles off shore just beyond a large floe of ice. If the **Chicora** or any other boat is out, stuck in the ice, as they may be in trying to cut through to the harbor, there is little hope for her or her crew tonight as no help can go to them, their only help, the **Tramp**, being fast in the ice with no hope for release. Great anxiety is felt for the **Chicora's** safety, as the company have no tidings from her up to 10 o'clock tonight.

The following day the *Free Press* would say briefly that, "Reports have been sent out that she was in sight of St. Joseph last night, but this was erroneous."

The **Ann Arbor No. 1** finally made port at Menominee in Michigan's upper peninsula near the Wisconsin border, just past 10 p.m. Monday night. She had been on the lake since leaving Frankfort, Michigan, at 1:30 a.m. Friday morning. There were fears raised in Milwaukee for the **Petoskey** which they thought had left St. Joseph.

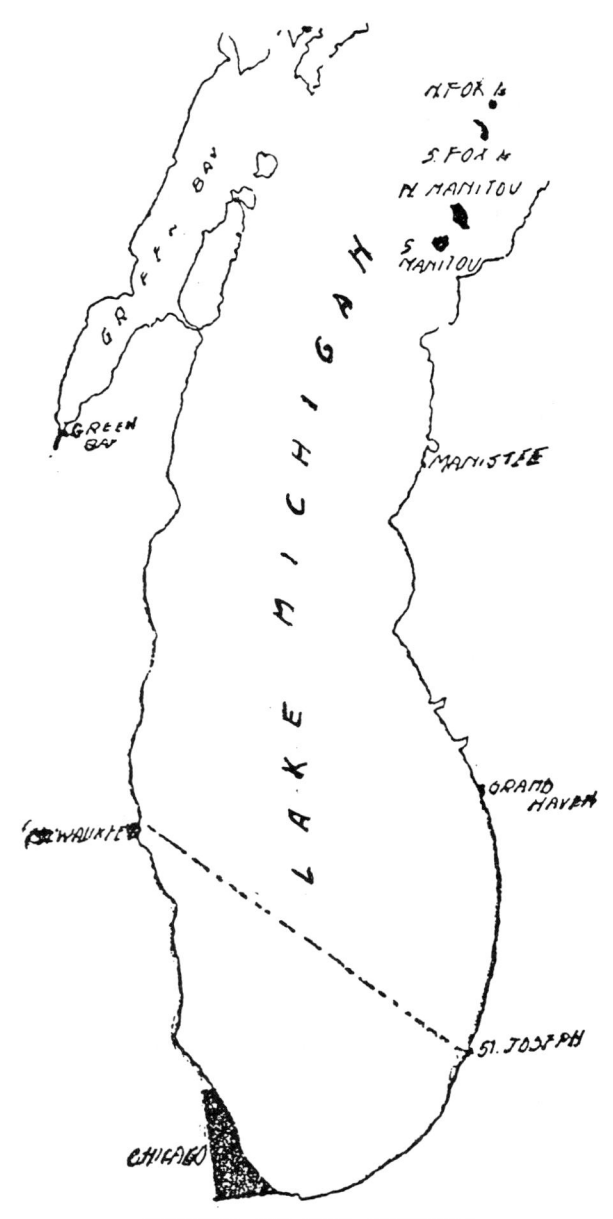

COURSE OF THE CHICORA.

The route from Milwaukee to St. Joseph was almost directly southeast. In ordinary circumstances the Chicora could make the distance in about six hours. This map, from the January 24 issue of the Chicago InterOcean shows the islands in northern Lake Michigan where many hoped the missing boat had sought refuge.

The **F & P. M. No. 4** had left Milwaukee three hours after the **Chicora** headed for Ludington with a full cargo of flour. About three hours out the vessel encountered such heavy weather that Captain Joseph Russell decided that even if he made it to the Michigan shore it would be impossible to cut through the ice field which would have been created by the gale. He turned back for Milwaukee at 11 a.m. and did not succeed in getting inside the harbor until after 10 p.m., laboring under a heavy coating of ice. He told a reporter that it was one of the severest gales which he had seen in his experience on the lakes and that on account of the blinding snow and high winds he found it hard to make the harbor at Milwaukee.

The tower of the Graham house on Broad Street, St. Joseph, gave the owner a vantage point to scan the horizon for the missing steamer.

4

Is No News Good News?

Tuesday, January 22

All day Tuesday it was vainly hoped that the missing vessel would be heard from. According to the *Chicago Tribune* "friends of the crew on the missing boat stood on the bluffs eagerly scanning the lake for a trace of smoke which might mark its location. They were unrewarded. They became anxious toward night, when they saw that the northwest gale which had been sweeping in from the lake all day was not to go down with the sun. Instead the mercury dropped ominously and fears for the missing steamer were greatly increased."

Graham responded to inquiries, the *Tribune* reporter noted, by professing the utmost confidence in the steamer's safety. "He believed the boat had been caught in an ice floe and would free itself and be in port by morning."

Provisions were carried over the ice to the crew of the fishing tug **Tramp** which had gotten stuck in the ice near the pier at St. Joseph Monday morning on her way out to tend nets.

By Tuesday night anxiety began to turn to fear. The company sent telegrams to ports on both sides of Lake Michigan and received replies:

NO SIGHT OF **CHICORA** HERE.

The Holland newspaper reported:

STILL OUT

At all ports along the lake where the boat by any possibility could touch or be sighted the company has men on watch, so that the news of the first glimpse of her can be wired at once to headquarters. Capt. Morton of the life saving station at Holland harbor has also been on the constant lookout, but reports that he has not sighted a vessel of any description during the storm, and that there is not much ice between here and Saugatuck.

NO TIDINGS AS YET OF THE MISSING CHICORA.

A DAY OF ANXIETY AT BENTON HARBOR AND ST. JOSEPH.

THOUGHT THE BOAT IS IN MIDLAKE, WAITING FOR FAIR WEATHER.

PRESIDENT GRAHAM THINKS NO NEWS IS GOOD NEWS.

> He is well acquainted with the master of the steamer, Capt. Ed. Stines, and also his son, who is second mate, and thinks that if any man could bring the steamer through it is Capt. Stines.
>
> At St. Joseph where the main office of the company is located, and where the families or the friends of nearly every member of the crew live, the anxiety is intense, and the superintendent's office has been crowded day and night with heart-broken people. . . . At the bluff all day long men and women are eagerly scanning the eastern horizon for a trace of the smoke which might mark the location of the steamer.

At Milwaukee, where the journey began, Graham & Morton agent Adolph Reichle said, "I do not despair of the safety of the **Chicora**. It is a good, strong boat and ought to easily weather a storm like yesterday's. It was built especially for the winter transportation business. I will not give up hope until the fog clears and a careful search had been made. Even if the boat is gone all hope for the safety of the crew is not despaired of, as it may be that they are afloat on the ice and can be rescued."

A telegram telling of the **Chicora's** disappearance had been sent by Graham to Andrew Crawford in Chicago. Crawford told reporters that the boat was not insured, but that it had been especially built for the winter trade and he had such confidence in the **Chicora** and its commander that he thought it would be found safe in an ice floe before many days.

The Goodrich steamer **City of Ludington**, commanded by Captain Henry Stines, brother of the **Chicora's** captain, left Chicago for Milwaukee Tuesday night with plans to keep a sharp lookout for any trace of the missing vessel. Captain Henry Stines said that it seemed likely to him that the machinery of the **Chicora** had somehow become disabled in the storm and the vessel was drifting in the lake.

When the *Detroit Free Press* went to press at 10 p.m. Tuesday night, they could only report in a short story:

> At 10 o'clock tonight nothing has been heard from the **Chicora**, and little hope is now entertained for her safety. Lighthouse keepers all up and down the lake on both shores are instructed to keep special watch during the night. The wind has increased in fury to a forty-five mile an hour velocity. Old sailors say that never has such a terrible wind storm swept the lake within their memory. The transportation company's officers look despondent and care to talk but little about the matter, fearing that the worst has happened, as much ice is floating all through the lake. There is no hope now of the **Petoskey** going out before daylight, as the sea is rolling as though it were mad.

The Wednesday Detroit newspapers reported that, "Mr. Graham president of the company, sat up nearly all night last night in the tower of his residence, the highest point of observation on the St. Joseph bluff, keeping watch for her lights, but saw none." The telegraph office was kept open until midnight, some reports said all night, but no news was received.

5

Wreckage at South Haven

Wednesday, January 23

The *Holland City News* reported, "J. H. Graham, president of the Graham & Morton line, continued up to Wednesday noon quite confident of the steamer's safety, relying upon the power and strength; he reasoned that the boat had been caught in an ice flow and would float round the lake until such time as the storm subsides and she can cut her way through the ice." The optimism was fueled by telegrams from Little Sable Point and Ludington, where boats "not usual in that vicinity" had been sighted early in the day.

Andrew Crawford later claimed that as early as Wednesday morning in response to a request from Graham he had tried to get a tug out of Chicago to search for the overdue vessel. Crawford said he had asked the Dunham Towing and Wrecking Company to dispatch one of their tugs to the rescue. "Mr. Dunham, president of the tug company, being out of town, nobody in their office was willing to take the responsibility sending a tug to the mercy of the waves and ice. Mr. Dunham was then communicated with by telegraph and asked to allow the tug to be sent. He replied by wire refusing to allow the tug to go. No further attempt was made to get a boat to go out after the refusal from the towing company There was no use trying to secure one from any other company. The fact of the matter is that it would be an utter impossibility for a tug to get through the masses of ice on the east shore of the lake."

The *Chicago Tribune* carried a story in the Thursday paper that a telegram had been received by the Dunham tug line asking terms for a tug to go in search of the **Chicora**. "Capt. Dunham replied that with the mercury below zero and the wind blowing a gale he did not think it safe to send one tug, but would send two that they might assist each other. The discovery of the wreckage off South Haven stopped further negotiations."

The *Chicago Times Herald* in its Thursday story, carried the statement from Crawford that a request for a tug from the Dunham Tug and Wrecking Company had been made Wednesday morning, but that the company had refused to send one out. Captain J. S. Dunham of the company was questioned by the reporter and said that "Mr. Crawford was certainly mistaken in regard to the Dunham Towing Company having refused to send a tug from Chicago to look for the **Chicora**. We would have sent a tug had we been asked. We could do it."

WRECKAGE!

FOUND AND BROUGHT ASHORE
AT SOUTH HAVEN.

BEEN IDENTIFIED AS BELONG-
ING TO THE CHICORA.

MEN BELIEVE THAT SHE
HAS GONE DOWN

The *Times Herald* article continued:

No Call Made for a Tug.

The Dunham Tug and Wrecking Company was prepared all day to send out a tug in search of the **Chicora**, as they do most of the business of the Graham & Morton people, but no call was made upon them for assistance. Captain Reeve and his associates in the local office of the Graham & Morton Company sat there helpless all day, although it was the freely expressed opinion of all concerned that if any aid was to be given the missing boat it should come from Chicago where there were one or two tugs fully equipped for the battle to be fought in crossing the lake.

At the weather bureau in the Auditorium Professor Moore's assistants had no hesitation in expressing the opinion that relief tugs could have cleared the Chicago harbor yesterday and reached the ice pack on the Michigan shore without much difficulty. If this had been done and the west edge of the pack cruised along the **Chicora**, providing she is not at the bottom of the lake, would have been sighted and communicated with by signals at least. The sixty-four mile gait of the wind on Monday and the thirty-mile clip on Tuesday, despite the cold, prevented new ice forming off the west shore and drove the old ice into the neck of the lake between Grand Haven and the Indiana shore. In there the **Chicora** is lured if the waves have not engulfed her.

Officials Not in Chicago

An unfortunate feature of the Graham & Morton line of boats is that during the winter months the real executive heads are not in Chicago, but at St. Joseph and Benton Harbor. Andrew Crawford, of the Lincoln Park board of commissioners, is financially interested in the line and is the only one of this side of the lake who could have been appealed to yesterday to send out a tug in search of the missing boat.

A wire had been received late Tuesday night that a vessel had been sighted off Racine, Wisconsin, but in the light of day the report was retracted. The Kalamazoo newspaper ran a wire report from St. Joseph which said in part: "Every clue is grasped and petted longingly until better judgment declares it an impossibility, when it is discarded. . . . The wives and mothers of the men who have probably gone to a watery grave did not close their eyes last night, but with sinking hearts and awful forebodings sat up all night anxiously waiting for some tidings from the missing steamer and the missing loved ones. . . . There is only a faint ray of hope for a little while at a time. All business at this point is secondary to the prevailing thought and conversation concerning the **Chicora**."

The *Benton Harbor Daily Palladium*, the newspaper that Morton would later be both stockholder and president of, and that was housed in the G & M building near the docks, held on with a fierce sort of optimism. In the issue that went to press just after 3 p.m. on Wednesday a story on the front page proclaimed:

THE CHICORA PROBABLY SAFE

>The *Palladium* shares the faith of the officers of the Graham & Morton Transportation Company and those best acquainted with the missing steamer **Chicora** and her trustworthy crew in the belief that the vessel has not foundered but is safe though helpless somewhere in mid-lake. She is doubtless either caught in an immense ice floe, which renders her propelling power useless, or she may have suffered some impairment of her machinery which makes her progress equally impossible. The boat was staunch enough to outlive even the terrific wind and angry sea which prevailed from Monday to Tuesday, and Capt. Stines was fully able to handle the steamer in any weather.
>
>Too much sensational speculations have been indulged in by the city newspapers and their correspondents and much needless alarm has been created. Until another forty-eight hours have gone by and the lake has been thoroughly scanned by the vessels sent out for the purpose, without satisfactory tidings, it is premature to presume that the **Chicora** has met with any serious disaster.

On pages inside the editor insisted:

>Hope is by no means abandoned, and there are plausible reasons to account for the vessel's obscurity from sight of land on either shore of Lake Michigan. . . . Arrangements are being or have been made by telegraph for tugs at Chicago and Ludington to be held in readiness to put to sea on short notice and go in search of the missing boat as soon as the weather will permit. At present it would be considered useless for a boat to go out as the weather is still very heavy and the air most of the time is filled with fine snow which would prevent a vessel from being seen at any distance. The captain of the car ferry steamer **No. 2**, which was to have left Frankfort today noon for Kewaunee, was instructed to make inquires for the **Chicora** at the Manitou Islands, which are directly on her route. Ferry **No. 1** was also expected at Frankfort today and there is some hope that her captain may have news of the **Chicora**.

The fierce storm on the Michigan shore had subsided some by Tuesday evening, although there was still a lot of wind and locally heavy snowstorms. The temperature remained bitterly cold. The storm had caused problems on the land as well and Wednesday morning many of the roads were still blocked by snowdrifts five and six feet deep.

Timothy Plummer, who owned a small farm in Casco Township, Allegan County, told reporters at South Haven, "This morning while coming to town the snow lifted for a few minutes, and I distinctly saw a large steamer outside the ice and apparently all right, but the snow set in again soon afterwards, and this is the last that has been seen of the steamer."

Ed Napier, who seems to have taken a personal interest in the tragedy from the very beginning, telegraphed the news from South Haven to Graham at Benton Harbor:

> MAN FROM COUNTRY NAMED TIMOTHY PLUMMER JUST CAME IN AND SAID HE SAW A BOAT AT 10 O' CLOCK THIS FORENOON SOME DISTANCE IN LAKE OFF A POINT ABOUT FIVE MILES NORTH OF HERE, HE ONLY SAW HER FOR A MINUTE.

With this positive possibility, watchers up and down the coast intensified their efforts. At 3 p.m. a telegram was sent to Benton Harbor from South Haven that reported a steamer fast in the ice five miles off South Haven, supposed to be the **Chicora**. This was quickly identified as false, although some searchers later tried to explain that what they had seen, and thought was an intact craft, was actually pieces of wreckage imbedded in the ice.

A report in the *Niles Weekly Mirror* gives to Charles Donahue, keeper of the South Haven lighthouse, credit for the discovery of the first wreckage.

> The anxious eyes of Light house Keeper Charles Donoghue, at South Haven, which have for days been looking to the west over the ice-bound lake for signs of the missing propeller **Chicora**, with her human freight, were rewarded on Wednesday afternoon, by discovering several miles out specks which, in the glass, were soon seen to be pieces of wreckage. They were only specks, but to the mariner's quick eye they told of the unquestionable loss of a vessel and all on board. The wreckage was about two miles out from shore, most of it directly opposite the harbor. The ice appeared to extend half a mile further out into the lake. Mariners at once organized a relief party to go out and investigate the wreckage. Captain Matthews, of the United States life saving service, led the party of searchers that braved the wintry wind blowing in their faces at a rate of upward of thirty miles and hour. The trip out from land was a perilous one, for the ice, while driven into a compact mass by the gale of the last two days, was still dangerous, and in places uncertain on account of its roughness and the liability of its breaking up.
>
> After two miles, which seemed to be ten, had been covered Capt. Matthews and his party came to a mass of wreckage imbedded in the ice, but apparently of a boat that had but recently met with disaster. There were a number of pieces that appeared to belong to the upper works of some large vessel, probably a propeller or steamer of some large line. Much of the wreckage was under the ice or water, which made it difficult to reach in order to closely describe. The men hunted around for pieces of the pilot-house, by which the name of the vessel could be learned, but they were unsuccessful. Portions of the wreckage were secured and carried back to the land, where

experienced seamen who knew the Graham & Morton vessel identified them as belonging to the **Chicora**.

Others out on the ice, according to the *South Haven Messenger*, were Will Spooner and Charles Rickley. One of the things they found was the roof of the hurricane deck. Rickley climbed up on top to assure himself that it was from the **Chicora**. He decided it was. A later newspaper reported that they had found "some pieces of the upper works of a steamer, known by certain peculiarities to have belonged to the **Chicora**." At 5: 30 p.m. Napier telegraphed Graham:

> WE HAVE JUST FOUND SOME OF THE **CHICORA'S** UPPER WORKS IN THE ICE OFF THIS PLACE. THERE IS NO DOUBT SHE HAS FOUNDERED. I AM JUST GOING FIVE MILES NORTH OF HERE TO SEE WHAT THERE IS THAT PLUMMER REPORTED THIS MORNING.

An 1895 map showing the small farm of T. Plummer at the northern edge of section 25, Casco Township, Allegan County. The outskirts of South Haven are seen in the lower left hand corner.

Finally even the *Benton Harbor Palladium* capitulated. The newspaper had carried Napier's first telegram concerning the sighting by Timothy Plummer in the regular edition. After the second telegram, about 6 p.m. the *Palladium* put out an extra with a new headline. This one shouted:

THE CHICORA LOST!

Part of Her Cabin Found off South Haven

Little Doubt that the Steamer Has Foundered

The next day the *Palladium* described the scene at Benton Harbor following the arrival of Napier's telegram about the wreckage:

> As this news spread over the city by word of mouth and the extra edition of *The Palladium* that was quickly made up and printed, fear was intensified and almost everybody gave up all hope for the vessel and lives of the men on board. Great excitement prevailed and from the time the telegram was received until late in the evening the offices of the Graham & Morton Transportation Co. and *The Palladium* were crowded with relatives and friends of those aboard the **Chicora** and others, all eager for any further news that might be received.

Captain Ed Napier of South Haven was well known both in Chicago and West Michigan. He was the son of Captain Nelson W. Napier who had been lost on the **Alpena** in 1880. He was at this time the owner of the steamer **Macatawa** which ran summer excursions in Chicago between the Randolph Street pier and Jackson Park. (The **Macatawa** would burn in a spectacular fire in Chicago the next September.) The *Chicago Tribune* noted that "Capt. Napier, who formerly lived in Chicago, is regarded as a perfectly trustworthy man and one of the most skilled seamen on the lake." He and Captain Stines were both aboard a sailing vessel about 1880 when it became frozen in the ice off St. Joseph harbor, and the two walked to shore together. He had received a number of life saving medals for rescuing people in peril in the ice of Chicago harbor. He was better known in western Michigan as the former owner and captain of the **Music** which ran excursions on Lake Macatawa near Holland until Napier was arrested in the summer of 1894 for selling liquor without a license.

For the rest of the night the telegrams continued to arrive. At about 6 p.m. the Western Union telegraph agent at South Haven wired the agent at Benton Harbor:

> THE UPPER DECK OF SOME STEAMER THAT HAS GONE TO PIECES LATELY WAS FOUND BY CAPT. BOYNE AND HIS MEN. THEY SAY IT WAS PAINTED BLACK, BUT NO NAME ON IT TO TELL WHAT BOAT IT IS FROM; BUT THEY THINK IT IS PART OF THE **CHICORA**.

Captain Napier, arrived back in South Haven, after tracking down Timothy Plummer, and at 7:30 p.m. sent a telegram which said:

> FORWARD PART OF BULWARKS AND WINDOWS IN SAME FOUND IN ICE OFF HERE. SAW PLUMMER; HE IS POSITIVE HE SAW A STEAMER AT 10 A.M. OUTSIDE OF ICE; SNOW SETTLED; COULD SEE NO MORE. HE IS A MAN WHO OUGHT TO KNOW. IT DON'T NECESSARILY FOLLOW THAT BOAT IS DOWN ON ACCOUNT OF THESE PIECES.

The manager of the Western Union office in South Haven, O. E. Harmon, wired shortly afterwards:

> WRECKAGE WAS DISCOVERED OPPOSITE THIS HARBOR THIS P.M. A PARTY HEADED BY CAPT. MATTHEWS OF THE LIFE SAVING STATION WENT OUT ON THE ICE AND FOUND PIECES OF THE UPPER WORK OF A STEAMER WHICH SOME IDENTIFIED AS PORTION OF THE **CHICORA**. DARKNESS STOPPED ALL FURTHER SEARCH. ABSOLUTELY NOTHING MORE CAN BE LEARNED UNTIL TOMORROW.

In response to the telegrams J. S. Morton and William J. Hancock, the regular clerk of the **Chicora** who had reached Benton Harbor too late to sail for Milwaukee with the boat, left by express train to Grand Junction and drove by sleigh to South Haven arriving there shortly after 11 p.m.. Reporter Ira A. Smith of the *Benton Harbor Palladium* accompanied them, reporter Moulton of the *St. Joseph Press* followed.

Probably while Morton and Hancock were still en route a telegraph message arrived in Benton Harbor from Captain John Boyne of South Haven, captain of the steamer **H. W. Williams**, who had headed one of the searching parties:

> THERE IS WRECKAGE ON THE OUTER END OF THE ICE OFF THIS PLACE FOR ABOUT TWO MILES AS NEAR AS WE CAN TELL. FOUND ALL OF THE UPPER DECK FORWARD BUT DO NOT FIND ANY OF THE CABIN. THICKNESS ONE INCH, LAP JOINT, BLACK OUTSIDE, LEAD COLOR INSIDE. THERE OUGHT TO BE SOME ONE HERE THAT KNOWS MORE ABOUT THE BUILD OF THE **CHICORA** THAN WE DO. HAVE A COPPER SCUPPER TWO INCHES LONG THAT WAS TAKEN OUT OF THE UPPER DECK.

According to the *Detroit Free Press* on receipt of this message Mr. Graham said, "That settles it. I recognize perfectly the parts described as part of the **Chicora**. She is gone. She could not lose these parts of her structure without going under."

The *Chicago Tribune* adds to the scene, "Capt. Graham, who was cheerful and confident until he read the telegram, dropped into a chair and buried his face in his hands. He summoned Capt. Griffin of the **Petoskey** and told him to go out for the **Chicora**, to give it succor or to end the terrible suspense as soon as he could possibly cut his way through the mountains of ice that are jammed in the harbor."

But Morton wasn't ready to give up. At 12:30 a.m. he sent a telegram from South Haven to Graham in Benton Harbor:

> HAVE TALKED WITH NAPIER, BOYNE AND OTHERS. THEY HAVE PIECES OF DECK CANVAS PAINTED LEAD COLOR, COPPER SCUPPERS AND FORWARD BULWARKS, PAINTED BLACK, ONE AND ONE-EIGHTH INCHES THICK, FOUR INCHES WIDE SHIP LAP AND SAY THERE IS CONSIDERABLE MORE ABOUT ONE

MILE OUT FROM THE PIERS. NO BOATS OR ANYTHING AFT OF THE PILOT HOUSE. THE MAN THAT REPORTED SEEING A STEAMBOAT THIS MORNING IS A SAILOR AND SAYS HE IS NOT MISTAKEN. IT LOOKS TO US FROM ALL WE CAN LEARN AS IF SHE HAD CARRIED AWAY SOMETHING FORWARD AND THAT THE BOAT IS ALL RIGHT YET. NOTHING MORE TO-NIGHT.

One of the most optimistic accounts was published by the *Chicago InterOcean* issue of January 24 under the headline:

NO ALARM FELT HERE

All day yesterday the local office of the Graham & Morton Transportation Company, at the foot of Wabash avenue, was besieged by queries as to the fate of the missing steamer **Chicora**. Locally there were little fears expressed as to its safety and ultimate arrival in some port. Captain Henry Stines, commander of the Goodrich Line steamer **Ludington** whose brother, presumably, was lost with the others in the foundered craft, left this port for Milwaukee Tuesday evening at 7 o'clock. He had heard of the apprehensions expressed in the press dispatches about the steamer of which his brother was in command, but did not appear to worry much. He had faith in the steamer, and he knew that his brother, better than any man who walks the quarterdeck of a winter boat, was experienced in navigating through ice floes and packs.

Lieutenant Blow, local chief of the United States Hydrographic Bureau, in the Masonic Temple, argued that the **Chicora** was safe in the ice somewhere between Michigan City and Little Point au Sable, on the east shore. The vessel, he made out, had left Milwaukee at 5:20 o'clock Monday morning. The wind, then from the west, was aiding the steamer along toward her destination. The ninety-five miles run diagonally across the foot of the lake with the wind astern, or nearly so, should be made in seven or eight hours. The norther did not set in until 10:30 o'clock, so that the steamer was well in toward the edge of the ice on the east shore when the wind began to blow. The ice had then already begun to cross her bow, but Lieutenant Blow hoped that she had gotten out of this drift all right and had made for the slush inshore. . . . Her cargo of flour tended to brace her sides and strengthen them in resisting the attacks of the fields of loose cakes crossing her path. . . The first blow of Monday morning, from the west, loosened the fields and started them off shore, where the norther, which set in some six hours later, drove up the lake and against the east shore between Michigan City and Point au Sable. When these became compact they extended from a line all the way from seven to ten miles off the land. If she became fastened in this manner there was nothing for her to do but wait until an easterly wind broke a channel open for her. If "nipped" in this condition the crew would then have had a chance to save their lives by taking to the ice and making for the shore.

6

Out on the Ice Floes

Thursday, January 24

Thursday morning more wreckage was brought in dispelling all doubt. "Some still think that the hull may be afloat," the *South Haven Messenger* commented "but there is really nothing in fact or probability to indicate that such is the case. Undoubtedly every man on board perished. It was a terrible storm and a terrible sea, which would swallow up anyone washed into it in a moment."

When he was an old man J. S. Morton recounted his memories of the trip to Allen Chesebro, owner of a resort just south of South Haven, as Chesebro reported the interview:

> Mr. Morton . . . rode to South Haven with a team and bob sleighs. He had to face the 15 below zero weather blowing from the lake. The windswept road was partly bare. After reaching South Haven he went to a hotel and picked six or eight men to make the trip on the lake. Seward Ross, Andy Curran, Tom Kime and others started out on the ice from the pier. After some distance from shore the men had to jump the floating cakes of ice both up and down. It was extremely dangerous.
>
> When they were a mile and a half out, opposite our place, the men began to find wreckage. Mr. Morton said it was from the lower cabin on the first deck. The men then started north. North of South Haven they found more wreckage. Flour in barrels, doors, mahogany casings, etc. That night it was all the men could do to make shore. They went to Hotel Columbus [in South Haven], and stood their overcoats on the floor, frozen stiff.

GONE DOWN

THE STEAMER CHICORA WITH ALL ON BOARD.

NEARLY THIRTY PERSONS LOSE THEIR LIVES.

WRECKAGE FOUND OFF SOUTH HAVEN IDENTIFIED.

OWNERS OF THE BOAT GIVE UP THEIR LAST HOPE.

THEY NOW ACKNOWLEDGE THAT SHE HAS GONE UNDER.

At 11:30 a.m., after a morning search, Morton wired Graham in Benton Harbor:

> WE ARE FINDING MORE WRECKAGE NORTH OF PIER AND ONE AND ONE-HALF MILES OUT FROM SHORE. HAVE FOUND CABIN CURTAINS, PARTITIONS BETWEEN STATE ROOMS, PIECES OF MAHOGANY AND BAGGAGE ROOM DOORS.
>
> WE HAVE FOUND, OUT ONE MILE FROM THE PIER IN THE ICE, PORT SIDE FORWARD, UPPER BULWARKS FIVE FEET WIDE BY TWELVE FEET LONG AND INSIDE SHUTTER TO PASSENGER GANGWAY. ALL BELONGED TO THE **CHICORA**.

Newspapers later reported, "As these messages were read to the anxious friends about the telegraph office, President Graham's voice wavered. At the last sentence he broke completely down and went immediately to his own office to wire the worst news of the surely ill-fated **Chicora** to the relatives of the members of the crew who live at a distance. No more hope remained." The Kalamazoo reporter wrote, "A scene of sadness and gloom prevails at the crowded offices of the Graham & Morton company. Every citizen walks with bowed head and saddened countenance."

One of the early finds by those on the ice at South Haven was described by the Kalamazoo reporter as "two windows of a peculiar pattern which were in the forward bulwarks of the lost vessel. No such windows are known to be in any vessel now on the lakes. This is regarded as conclusive evidence by experienced lake men that the **Chicora** has gone to the bottom of Lake Michigan."

Relatives of the missing men began to gather. William McClure, engineer of the **City of Chicago** and brother of Robert McClure who was the first engineer aboard the **Chicora**, came from Detroit arriving by train at 3 a.m. Thursday. A son of the lost engineer arrived on the afternoon train. By evening train the search parties at South Haven were joined by Mrs. Pearl, wife of the passenger, her brother E. W. Cadwell; George Hummiston, Harry Wilson, William Russell, the regular second mate aboard the vessel, and Mr. Tibbits. Other newspapers reported that Mrs. Stines, whose husband and son were among the missing, and Mrs. Clarke, wife of the clerk, were also at South Haven. The *Palladium* reported, "Mrs. Pearl stands the great strain with fortitude and has made up her mind that her husband is lost. She went down on the pier this afternoon with Messrs. Cadwell and Hummiston and with glasses viewed what she could of the wreckage."

In the afternoon reporter Smith of the *Palladium* sent a wire that must have been carried ashore by another searcher:

> WE ARE STILL OUT ON THE ICE, FINDING MUCH WRECKAGE. WE ARE BEGINNING TO FIND THE WORKS AFT AND PARTS OF THE CABIN. THEY FOUND A BARREL OF FLOUR AND A DOOR FROM THE AFTER PART OF THE CABIN. A SEARCHING PARTY STARTED SOUTH AND WE ARE WORKING NORTH WHERE THE ICE IS COVERED WITH WRECKAGE. THE BAGGAGE ROOM DOOR HAS BEEN FOUND. IT IS LOOKING A LITTLE DARKER FOR US. A BLINDING SNOW STORM IS RAGING. WE HAVE COVERED SEVERAL MILES IN ALL. THEY FOUND SOME STATE-ROOM PARTITIONS.

And as the deadline approached a message received from reporter Smith at 2:15 p.m. was added to the previously organized news about the lost vessel. It was printed in the *Benton Harbor Daily Palladium* under the headline:

VERY LATEST

Farther north we found the social hall curtain with the hook to hold the passenger gangway shutter up, which was cut in half, this being from the solid work, and goes to show the hull must have gone to pieces above the main deck. This is the strongest evidence yet. Also found parts of drawing rooms 27 and 28. Another large piece of strong work was found, thought to be part of the baggage room or parcel room, though it could not be identified by Mr. Hancock as to exact location in the boat.

They walked so far that first day that reporter Smith wrote later that he "wore out my pair of rubbers before we returned. It was very hard walking as the ice is all chunks." By 3 p.m. the snow had canceled all further searching and Morton took the train to Benton Harbor arriving at 3:50 p.m. He carried several boards, doors, casings and pieces of wood coming from the cabin and upper deck. A crowd greeted him as he arrived at the train station "anxious to get a sight of this evidence of the awful disaster." He reported wreckage floating under the ice and within the slush and many large pieces farther out, "rising and falling with every billow as it rolls inward."

According to the Friday *Palladium* the pieces Morton brought were "recognized by President J. H. Graham as having been torn from the **Chicora**. That little bundle of wreckage spoke more eloquently than any words that could be framed of the fearful fate that had overtaken the steamer and her precious load of human lives."

Hancock and Smith were left in South Haven to continue the search, but Morton apparently brought back to Benton Harbor another story written by Smith of the day's adventure, for later editions. It carried the date line, "South Haven, Jan. 24, 3:20 p.m."

Have just returned from the ice. Mr. Morton has gone home. Mr. Hancock and myself will stay and go north tomorrow in search of bodies. We started at 7 a.m. at South Haven and found some of the forward upper bulwarks; went farther north and came upon lots of wreckage. Have found pieces from the top to lower deck, most of baggage room, upper shutter and one life preserver, but it did not have name on it; was torn. Found one barrel of flour one and a half miles north, which came from the cargo; it was broken. Some of the doors and cabin bulkheads are found, supposed to be from room 43, which was near the closet. Much wreckage is in sight farther to the north, but our party are so tired that we have had to give up till morning. There is no doubt that the **Chicora** is lost.

A lady stopping at the hotel claims to have seen a steamer off this port Monday afternoon at 2 o'clock.

From heavy wreckage lodged in ice it is thought the forward bulwarks went first, the cabin next and first deck next. Large crowds are on the ice looking for wreckage.

The *Grand Haven Evening Tribune* reported that the **Nyack** had finally worked her way out of Muskegon harbor late Thursday night and started up toward South Haven in the hope of finding the **Chicora**. However the vessel stranded in the ice three miles from Muskegon and disgruntled passengers later walked ashore. The **Nyack** remained stuck until a lull in the continuing storm finally permitted her to return to Muskegon on February 7.

A dark object had been seen about 10 miles out off Michigan City, Indiana. The newspaper wrote, "This end of the lake has been covered today with ice floes and the dark object was at the outer edge of the ice fields. It has not been identified positively as a boat or part of a boat and may be merely an iceberg. An effort this afternoon to make more accurate observations was prevented by a blinding snowstorm."

Graham wired the owners of the tug **Crosby** asking them to send the tug out to coast along the shore in search of the missing steamer. But the new storm made the trip unfeasible. According to the Benton Harbor newspaper he also hired James Pearl and a force of men to break a channel with dynamite through the thick ice in the harbor at St. Joseph. This was tried but shifting winds made it ineffective.

In Terre Haute, Indiana, officials of the Vandalia railroad which had several carloads of freight aboard the **Chicora** received a telegram from South Haven, "Port side and forward upper bulwarks, five feet wide and twelve feet long, and inside shutters to passenger gangway, all belonging to the **Chicora** were found this morning about a mile out in the ice." Vandalia secretary George Farmington was quoted as saying that the officials had become convinced that the boat had foundered.

In Chicago Andrew Crawford, described in the newspaper as the "principal owner of the **Chicora**," issued this statement:

> There was no insurance and the loss to the company will be about $175,000, but our greatest regret is the loss of life. It is dreadful to think that so many lives have been lost. Capt. Stines was a particularly fine fellow, able and courteous. I knew him well. He had been with the company some twenty-odd years and knew the lakes as well as any captain in the service.
>
> I do not blame him for the wreck of the **Chicora**, and yet it seems as though if he had studied his barometer Monday morning he would have known the storm was coming. The storm signals, however, I have learned were not displayed in Milwaukee for three hours after the boat had left that port.
>
> The gale must have struck the boat about 9 o'clock. If Capt. Stines had put into port or turned back all would have been well, but I suppose he thought it would blow over and kept on. I calculate the **Chicora** must have been within ten or twelve miles of St. Joseph when she was caught in the ice.
>
> What happened then will probably never be known. However it is easy to say what might have been. That Capt. Stines did his duty and guided his boat to the best of his knowledge, I have not the slightest doubt.
>
> The second mate, Bennie Stines, was an only son of the captain. Mrs. Stines is left alone at the family home at St. Joe.

Note: The Steamer Chicora was lost with a crew of 25 men while crossing from Milwaukee to St. Joseph Monday August 21, 1895 – She left Milwaukee at 5:45 A.M. that date ". Value of vessel and cargo $150,000.00 The steamer was in command of Capt. Edward Stines, C. A. Simons first mate – Robt. McClure Chief Engineer Jas. R. Clarke, Clerk. The steamer was never heard from or sighted after she left Milwaukee and all on board perished.

Benton Harbor Michigan.
January 24th 1895 –
The Stockholders met pursuant to adjournment. There being no quorum present, the meeting adjourned.

Fred A. Hobbs, Sec'y.

Secretary Fred A. Hobbs records the adjourned meeting of the Graham & Morton stockholders in the company minute book, but writes the wrong month in noting the loss of the **Chicora** *and the error was never corrected.*

He also told one Chicago reporter that the winter business between Milwaukee and St. Joseph had never proved profitable, but the company had been forced into it by competition.

The annual meeting of the Graham & Morton Co. had been held January 2, 1895, in Chicago. Crawford, who may have been the only one present except for Fred A. Hobbs, who served as secretary, voted his 151 shares and Graham's 150 shares, electing Graham, Crawford and Morton to the board of directors. The meeting was then adjourned to be reconvened January 24, 1895, at Benton Harbor.

A note on the next page of the official record book, written by Hobbs and datelined Benton Harbor, January 24, 1895, states, "The stockholders met pursuant to adjournment. There being no quorum present the meeting adjourned."

Between the two records in the minute book is a note, also in the handwriting of secretary Hobbs:

> Note: The Steamer **Chicora** was lost with a crew of 25 men while crossing from Milwaukee to St. Joseph Monday August 21 1895. She left Milwaukee at 5^{45} A.M. that date. Value of vessel and cargo $150,000.^{00} The steamer was in command of Capt. Edward Stines, CD Simons first mate, Robt McClure Chief Engineer Jas R. Clarke, clerk. The steamer was never heard from or sighted after she left Milwaukee and all on board perished.

Hobbs wrote August where he meant January, and was apparently too rattled to catch the error. It was never corrected.

Smith sent one last telegram from South Haven at 5:18 p.m. Thursday:

> CAPT. LEW MATHEWS OF THE LIFE SAVING CREW AND HIS SEARCHING PARTY HAVE FOUND FORWARD SPAR AND PIECE WITH PART OF **CHICORA'S** NAME ON IT.

At 10 p.m. Thursday night a piece of bulwark timber with lettering on it was brought in. The fragment included the letters "St. J" and was part of the words "St. Joseph and Benton Harbor" which were painted on all of the Graham & Morton boats.

7

Quick Look by Yawl

Friday, January 25

On Friday more than 400 searchers explored the frozen lake off South Haven hoping to find bodies of crew members who might have lashed themselves to a life preserver or a piece of timber before the vessel sank. They would have lived only a very short time in the zero winds and near-freezing lake, but a buoyed body might be found floating in the outer edge of the ice field. A Chicago newspaper explained that W. J. Hancock had been sent to South Haven because "Mr. Hancock is familiar with the face, apparel, and personal effects of the dead."

There was a misunderstanding in a wire from South Haven and at least one Chicago newspaper reported that 200 persons had been carried out on the ice. The *Inter Ocean* stated, "No one thus far has been in danger for one minute while searching or walking along the shore of ice."

Captain Matthews of the lifesaving station brought in the foremast, broken off even with the deck. One man found a huge piece of timber bearing the name **Chicora**, others discovered the steam chest from the kitchen and parts of the staterooms. Parts of the cabin and cargo were found floating in slush ice. Also discovered on Friday was the first barrel of flour, and a cabin bulkhead.

A reporter at South Haven wired the *Kalamazoo Daily Telegraph*:

Today is cold and dreary. The thermometer this morning was down to zero and the winds from the lake are freezing cold. But the brave party of searchers started out early as usual and tramped for miles along the shore and on the fields of ice. More pieces of the wreckage were found, ice-covered, and sometimes so deeply imbedded in the frozen mass as to require vigorous blows of the axe to release them. This town has not been so mournful for years. A pall seems to be over the whole place, for all

HELPLESS!

NO SEARCH CAN BE MADE FOR THE LOST CHICORA.

BOATS AFRAID TO PUT OUT IN THE STORM.

TERRIFIC GALES MAKING IT IMPOSSIBLE TO DO SO.

A WILD RUMOR THAT THE BOAT WAS SAFE.

realize that some where out in the frozen waters are the stiff and ghastly bodies of the ill fated crew of the **Chicora.**

Friday a volunteer crew carried a yawl boat a mile over the ice fields to open water. The party included Captain Boyne, Captain Matthews, Martin Hopkins, Charles Rickley, W. J. Russell, Adam Weckler, Art Wood, Fred Bentley, R. Lull, W. J Hancock and Ira Smith. According to an account later in the *Palladium:*

> They carried the boat on their shoulders over the rough ice with considerable difficulty to the edge of the field, where they launched the boat and in a comparatively smooth sea started to the northward to search for wreckage. After being out half an hour the sea began coming up and the party started to return, the rising waves, increasing wind and floating ice making this part of the trip very dangerous and difficult. It took an hour and a half to get back to solid ice and the people in the boat, as on-shore, meantimes grew very anxious. When the boat was landed it was covered with ice inside and out and the clothing of the occupants was likewise wet and frozen.

About 3 p.m. Friday the wind began to pick up and by midnight "as severe a gale as Monday's" was upon them. A foot of snow fell, drifting badly and impeding traffic on both land and water.

Friday, assisted by generous doses of dynamite, the tug **Tramp** was finally released from the ice near the harbor's mouth where she had languished since the previous Monday. She worked several hours breaking away the ice and opening up a channel to clear water outside the harbor, but was unable to go out onto the lake because of the weather and also because her long confinement in the ice had left her low on fuel. Before she could be refueled the wind shifted and drove the loose ice back into the mouth of the harbor.

The *St. Joseph Daily News* reported, "The wives and families of the lost seamen are frantic with grief. They have given up all hope, and now scan the fields of ice waiting for tidings of the remains of their loved ones."

Some of the Thursday papers, searching for news had reported that the wife of Captain Stines was "insane from grief" over losing both her husband and son. The Friday *Kalamazoo Daily Telegraph* described this report as "utterly false. The little woman is bearing up bravely. When the dispatch was received at the company's office yesterday afternoon that portions of the cabin of the **Chicora** had been found and that President Graham had given up, Mrs. Stines was in the office and wept bitterly. The scene in this office all day yesterday can better be imagined than described. It was heart rending."

The weather finally abated sufficiently for the mail carrier from South Manitou island to get to Glen Haven, and he reported that he had not seen the **Chicora** or any sign of wreckage.

8

A Committee Takes Action

Saturday, January 26

Citizens demanded that the Graham & Morton company send out rescue parties. According to the *Chicago Tribune* for January 27, there was a mass meeting held Saturday at Howard & Pearl's drug store in St. Joseph:

> Today they started a subscription paper to raise money to hire tugs to go and look for what may be found of the missing **Chicora**. They still hold to the belief that the hull of the **Chicora** has not gone down. If it is still afloat, either drifting or lodged somewhere in an ice field, they say there can be no doubt there are bodies on it, and unless the men perished of cold and hunger during the terrible weather that has raged on the lake ever since Monday they are still alive. In the absence of proof positive that the lives of those on the **Chicora** were lost their relatives and friends cling to the hope that some one may yet remain on the missing boat to tell the story of the terrible storm that has strewn miles of the coast with fragments of the boat's upper works. It is freely given out by old boatmen that the failure of the company to send a tug in search of the **Chicora** Thursday or Friday, when the weather would have permitted, was inexcusable neglect.

Captain Nelson Napier of St. Joseph accused the company of not sending tugs on Thursday or Friday because they were unwilling to pay the $12 an hour cost. The Rev. H. W. Davis, pastor of the Congregational Church of St. Joseph which was attended by the Stines, Pearl and Clarke families, was named chairman of the committee, and the subscription paper was drawn up, but no subscriptions were taken. It was clear even to the people at the meeting that nothing could be accomplished Saturday because of the new blizzard. The committee thought it best to wait until after a meeting with Graham on Sunday.

MOURNING!

MANY FAMILIES IN DESPAIR OVER THE LOSS OF THE CHICORA.

ELEVEN OF HER CREW WERE RESIDENTS OF DETROIT.

NAMES OF EIGHT OF THEM—DECK-HANDS—CANNOT BE LEARNED.

MORE WRECKAGE OF THE LOST BOAT FOUND AT SOUTH HAVEN.

The *Tribune* reporter went on to say that, "Many people refused to talk, saying the Graham & Morton Transportation company dominates the two cities and they could not afford to incur its ill-will." The meeting received little coverage from the local newspaper but an account of it ran nearly a column long on the front page of the *Chicago Tribune* and it received good play in the Detroit newspapers.

The *Detroit Free Press* reported: "A bitter feeling is being worked up among many citizens at St. Joseph because Mr. Graham has not sent some assistance from some point or other to rescue, if possible the men who might still be drifting helplessly around penned in the hold of the **Chicora** and possibly still alive. Any such feeling would soon be dispelled if they were personally acquainted with Mr. Graham or knew of the efforts he has already made to send assistance to the scene. When all other plans proved fruitless Mr. Graham ordered a crew to work clearing St. Joseph harbor to let the tug **Tramp** and the steamer **Petoskey** out, but before the channel was hardly open to the sea a strong gale was blowing from east as ever came from the west, lashing the seas into a terrible fury, making it utterly impossible for any boat to weather the seas."

The offshore winds made the terrain even more dangerous for the searchers. As the *Detroit Free Press* for January 26, 1895, explained:

> Heavy winds coming off land blew everything far out into the lake, breaking up the immense ice fields all up and down the shore for many miles. Several of the searchers barely got off the ice fields with their lives, great chunks of ice breaking off under their feet, they being obliged to jump across the open water to the ice time and again, running, stumbling, jumping from block to block, keeping up the race for their own lives for half an hour or more. The heavy gale that blew everything from the shore started it in the right direction to drift opposite St. Joseph where the later veering of the winds would drive it ashore, scattering it along the beach for a score of miles.

Unable to continue their work in the high winds and storm Hancock and Russell who had been organizing the search for bodies and wreckage at South Haven, and reporter Smith returned by train to Benton Harbor carrying with them the clerk's door and a bed rail.

With a lull in actual news the *Benton Harbor Daily Palladium* had space to rail at newspapers that they felt were not covering the story in a responsible manner:

> It is passing strange that the newspapers so generally and so indiscriminately accept and publish ridiculously false reports about current happenings. For the sake of being sensational or of feeding a morbid curiosity with anything it will swallow. . . it is scarcely a wonder that the remark is growing so common and so widely believed that "you cannot believe what you read in the newspapers now-a-days."
>
> The alleged portrait of Capt. Edward Stines which has been printed in Grand Rapids, Kalamazoo and other papers does not look at all like him. . . The picture probably was made for some one else. . . . Pictures have also been printed of the **Chicora** but they do not in any case look like that boat.

THE CHICORA.

STEAMER CHICORA.

THE STEAMER CHICORA, MISSING SINCE JAN. 21.

Some newspapers illustrated the news of the Chicora with any kind of boat drawing they had handy in their files.

A large portion of the *Daily Palladium* editor's disdain was reserved for what it called:

THAT DOG STORY

The story of a dog having swam ashore from the **Chicora** near Riverside is going the rounds of the papers, but like many other foolish things that have been printed the story is a fake pure and simple. The dog in question is a grizzly canine known by the name of "Rough" that has hung around the Big Four depot and G & M docks here for several months, and it is known that the cur has been here every day since the **Chicora** sailed on her last trip from this port.

But others, sensing a good story, were not so swift to dismiss the tale. Arriving in Benton Harbor by train on Saturday was a snuff-colored skye terrier that was reported to have been discovered Tuesday night, whining at the door of a road house at Pottowattomie Park, a summer resort eight miles north of Benton Harbor. The dog was "half-starved, half frozen" according to the finder, and literally covered with ice.

The animal was taken to the Graham & Morton docks and recognized by workers as an dog that was frequently aboard the boats. Although several newspapers reported that the workers were not absolutely certain that the animal had been aboard the **Chicora** when the vessel left for Milwaukee, January 20, the *Chicago Tribune* reported in a front page story published in the January 28 issue:

The dog was immediately recognized by the stevedores who work on the Graham docks and by the crew of the **Petoskey** as the animal that was aboard the **Chicora** when it left. The dog has been a tramp passenger on the Graham & Morton Transportation company's boat for several months. It has been dividing its time between the **Chicora** and the **Petoskey** this winter. No one claims ownership of it, and the nearest friend of the animal is Capt. Griffin of the **Petoskey**, who has been kinder to it than any one else. Since the dog became a passenger on these boats it has never missed a trip, taking the first boat to leave. As soon as the gangway would be let down, the sailors say, it would immediately spring ashore and disappear. When the boat was ready to leave the little fellow would be on hand again. This peculiarity about the animal has made it familiar to the people here of the two towns. It is an ill kempt looking little fellow, weighing about eight pounds.

The editor for the *Kalamazoo Evening Telegraph* was also a believer. The paper reported in the January 28 issue:

No one claims the animal, in fact he acts as though he had no friends now. The poor creature seems dazed and wags its tail pathetically and shivers when spoken to. He is doubtless the only survivor of the awful tragedy. The return of the animal indicates that the **Chicora** was within a half mile of the east shore Tuesday evening, the second night out. The dog, it is believed, could not swim more than one-quarter mile.

Many were skeptical. The editor of the *Three Oaks Press* sniffed in the February 1 issue: "The story of a snuff colored dog, which swam from the **Chicora** ashore, although printed in all the papers is now branded a fairy tale. The dog, as a matter of fact, did not go out on the boat, but stayed about the docks." The *Berrien Springs Journal Era* editorialized, "The number of people who were not on the **Chicora**, owing to some trifling circumstance over which they had no control, would have sunk the boat anywhere. . . Even a dejected looking dog at Benton Harbor is trying to make people believe he walked ashore from the wreck."

The following week the *Palladium* published a letter to the editor from Solon Cutler of Pottawatomie Park, at whose door the dog was supposed to have arrived. He wrote, "I received a dispatch today from Kohn & Middleton of Chicago, wanting to hire or buy the dog received from the steamer **Chicora**. I wish to say there was no dog came to my place as reported, and I knew nothing about the story until I learned it was going the rounds of the papers. Some one must have a very vivid imagination."

Another dog, possibly related to the wreck, was described by Margaret (Umphrey) Fullriede in a January 1988 letter to the *Benton Harbor News-Palladium*. She wrote that her father, Simon Frank Umphrey, who was then about 8, found a dog that came to a tavern in Coloma in a very bedraggled and weakened condition after the sinking. He nursed the animal backed to health and the grateful dog remained with the family for many years.

Exactly how the **Chicora** went down has been the subject of speculation since January 21, 1895. An early official version, was offered by the *Detroit Free Press*, for January 26:

> In conversation with J. H. Graham and two other officers of the company, they advanced the following theory as the most plausible as to the manner in which the steamer **Chicora** met her fate: That while turning to run back, head into the waves, and while still on the quarter making the turn, mountains of water and ice struck her forward of the bulwarks carrying away part of the cabin near the bow, and then, being partially disabled made from three to five miles before broken up any more of consequence. When opposite South Haven, probably thirty miles out, she lost first the stern part of her cabin, then soon after everything amidships was knocked off and leaving her with no protection from the waves that rolled over her thousands of times til everything was full of water, when she sunk to the bottom with the greater part of her cargo and all of the men that had not been knocked off previously and drowned, if not killed by the immense mountains of ice tumbling over and through her.

That week's *Grand Haven Evening News*, a port on Lake Michigan at the mouth of the Grand River, considered the question:

The most plausible theory in regard to the probable course taken by the ill-fated steamer **Chicora**, last Monday during the terrible storm that sealed the fate of the magnificent vessel and all on board, and the one that seems to find most favor with leading steamboat men, is that she came within from ten to twenty miles of Benton Harbor, and finding it useless to try to make port there, Capt. Stines put about and headed for the west shore and drifted to a point nearly opposite South Haven, where the steamer foundered and went to pieces. From the distance out in the floating ice at which the wreckage was picked up it is calculated that the steamer must have been very near mid-lake when she was wrecked.

Fifty years later Captain Oscar Bjork, veteran master of the **City of Grand Rapids**, having discussed it with those who had sailed on her said, "She was a crank boat. Captain William Russell, who sailed her often, told me that she was hard to handle, especially in a southwest gale. She was loaded with flour on her lower decks and it's possible that the cargo shifted and broke loose. A bad gale was blowing and it's my opinion Captain Stines found himself in the trough of the sea. The **Chicora** was high and narrow of beam. She probably rolled over and then went down fast."

On Saturday, January 26, Graham also made the announcement that boats of the line would continue their work as soon as it was feasible to get out on the lake and that there would be no delay carrying freight for the Big Four Railway other than that forced upon them by the weather. Work would be rushed on the **R. C. Reid** which had been put into dry dock at the end of the fall season to be lengthened, and the **Reid**, along with the **Petoskey** would be able to take care of the winter freight, with the **City of Chicago** joining them as soon as the floating ice was out of the lake. He issued a brief statement, "It may be depended on that the company will be fully equipped in due season to take care of all the business that may come their way."

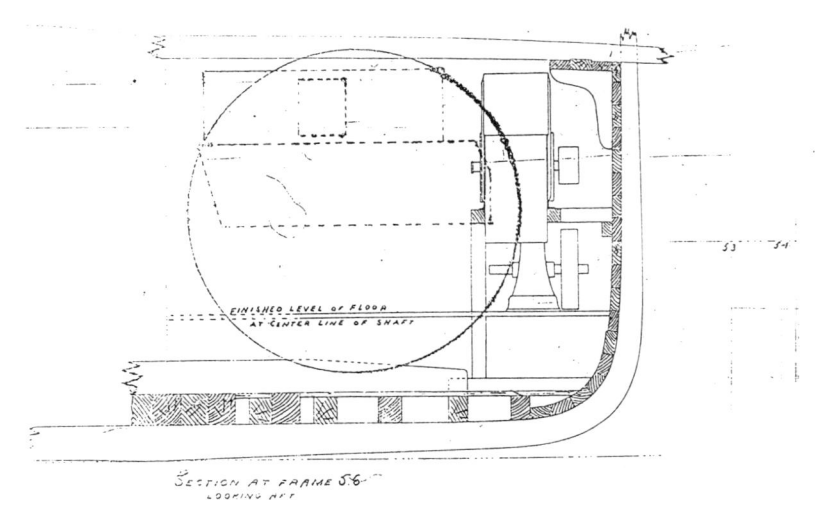

A midship cross section from the builder's plan of the Chicora.

9

A Storm-Forced Interlude

Sunday, January 27

One reporter, identified in the paper simply as "Ros." arrived in South Haven hoping to accompany the searchers on their rounds Sunday. Because of the storm there was little action but he later filed a long story with the *Kalamazoo Daily Telegraph* describing the scene:

> The lake front at this point and for miles in each direction north and south, presents about as desolate, forbidding and angry an appearance as could be possibly imagined. Looking out on the lake in any direction nothing can be seen but ice, rough jagged ice, in small lumps and monster chunks strewn together promiscuously, piled up in great heaps and frozen solidly together except for here and there a patch of black open water which refuses to submit to the bitter cold . . . I ventured out on the lake Sunday afternoon . . . The course I followed led from the Columbus House to the river, across to the life saving station, along the north pier, across the river again to the light house, out about a mile on the lake, a half mile to the south and back to the hotel. This trip of about three miles took two hours and a half to accomplish.
>
> From the hotel window, no idea of the storm could be gained; the swirling snow the fierce gusts of wind, the few pedestrians and the absolute lack of vehicles of any kind showed that there was a storm, but it was not until one stepped outside where the wind had a clean sweep from the lake, that the true forces were realized, and, when the river was reached the wind, without obstruction of any kind, swept in with a power that was almost irresistible. It was a laborious undertaking to cross the river, but it was accomplished at last without any serious accident and once within the shelter of the Life Saving station, whose heavy timbers defied the elements, the wild storm outside would have been forgotten but for the screech and moaning of the wind and the slight tremble of the building. . . . Capt. Matthews, the keeper, was at home and showed me, half frozen, a seat beside a roaring stove, near which in a little pile were some of the relics of the foundered steamer picked up by the searching party which tempted Providence in an open boat last week. There was a square piece of plush which the captain said had been attached to a portion of a chair when found, a piece of canvass from the upper deck, a locker door and a truck through which the signal halyards had

been rove. They all showed by the deep scars and dents the crushing power of the ice, and the truck, which was made of the hardest known wood, was cracked and battered as though made of tin.

The captain was surprised at the long continuance of the storm, but said that according to his barometer indications a change for the better could be expected at once. He said that he heard nothing and saw nothing on the night of the disaster, and had he, it is doubtful if any aid could have been rendered, although the attempt would have been made. . . .

The treacherous nature of the ice is not apparent until one ventures upon it, what appears to be a rough but solid surface being filled with snow covered air holes, which in some cases are large enough to admit the body of a man. Should a person fall into one of these, even though with a party, he would never live to tell the tale, for the ice cold water would numb him before he could cry out. In spite of this danger a party has been formed which on the first fair day will spend several hours in a search for something which will settle for a certain the primary cause of the **Chicora's** loss.

The general opinion here is that the wreck lies about two miles off South Haven to the north in perhaps twelve fathoms of water. Should this prove true the boat will not change her position and can be raised in the spring.

The piers at South Haven showing the U. S. Life Saving Service watch tower on the north pier and a lighthouse on the south pier. This steel lighthouse replaced a earlier wooden structure in 1903. The life saving tower was moved in 1908.

The **Chicora** was news even in newspapers away from the Great Lakes. The January 23 *New York Times* had carried a notice about the missing vessel and on Saturday, January 27, carried a small story announcing the discovery of wreckage. Most of the report was collected by wire and the vessel **Petoskey** was wrongly called the **Peter Key** in the article probably because the wire operator was unfamiliar with the Indian word.

> ### THE WRECK OF THE CHICORA.
>
> #### It Is Now Believed the Members of the Crew Were Frozen to Death.
>
> BENTON HARBOR, Mich., Jan. 26.—Reports are still coming in of the finding of immense piles of wreckage of the steamer Chicora. President Graham thinks every man was frozen at his post. Monday morning, on account of the low barometer, he told the Captain of the Peter Key to remain here with his boat, and also wired Capt. Stines in Milwaukee, but received a reply that the vessel had already left. The Chicora had been stripped of all her cabin furniture, carpets, piano, &c., before being placed in Winter service. A Muskegon dispatch states that the steamer Nyack left there yesterday for Milwaukee, to make a circuitous route in search of the Chicora wreck.
>
> Mrs. Pearl, the wife of the only passenger on the Chicora, has become insane from the shock caused by the loss of her husband.

The New York Times for January 27, 1895, carried an account of the sinking of the **Chicora**, *but the telegraph operator was apparently unfamiliar with the name* **Petoskey**.

On Sunday wreckage was discovered near Saugatuck. A letter sent to Graham Sunday afternoon from Frank Hancock details their expedition:

> Two men have just come in from the ice with pieces undoubtedly from the **Chicora** and reporting a piece as large as a house. The weather being so bad they were there only a few minutes, but report the ice being covered with pieces and fragments of wood as far as they could see. A party of us are going out in the morning if the weather permits, and I will report to you if we discover anything of importance. One piece brought in is thought to be a circle around the receiver on the engine to which the jacket is fastened. Another piece is circular in shape with veneer attached and there is also a

piece of inch stuff from a bulkhead or something similar. This was found on the edge of the ice about two miles out from Reed's point, it being quite dangerous to get to.

Reid's point, near a lakeshore farm owned by Captain Robert Reid, is just south of present-day 130th Avenue in Saugatuck Township, Allegan County, west and south of the Village of Douglas.

Reid's Point at the north edge of section 20, Saugatuck Township, Allegan County.

9

Masts Found Near Douglas

Monday, January 28

Because of the continuing storm all of the searching for the lost boat and possible survivors had to be done from shore. This angered family and friends of the deceased who wanted, at least, prompt recovery of the bodies. The *Berrien Springs Journal Era* tried to sort things out, "Her loss must be attributed to the phenomenal storm that prevailed that day. There is no use in blaming the owners of the boat, who were ashore, for they were ready, in their own interest if not in the interest of humanity, to do all in their power to save life and property. It is probable that the bad work was done before they could have done a thing to help the boat. Indeed, no other boat on the lake could have lived outside that day, and by the time that it became apparent that the boat was in trouble she was, in all probability, lost beyond help."

According to the January 28 issue of the *Benton Harbor Daily Palladium*, Graham, goaded by the citizen committee, renewed his efforts to get a tug Monday morning:

> Mr. Graham has been untiring in his efforts to get boats to go out into the lake in search of whatever may be afloat of the wrecked **Chicora**, keeping in constant communication with the towing companies and tug owners at the several lake ports. This morning he talked with the Dunham Towing Co. of Chicago, by telephone and also sent the company a telegram urging them to send out a tug. The reply in both cases was that the company would not send one tug out alone under any circumstances, and would not send two tugs until the weather cleared up.

On Monday watchers straining their eyes and glasses lakeward from the St. Joseph bluff thought that they actually saw the long-awaited tug far out into the lake, but further investigation revealed that the shape which had been mistaken for a tug was actually a large hummock of ice drifting along the outer edge of the frozen field.

In the afternoon, frustrated by his inability to persuade someone to send a rescue vessel, Graham ordered the **Petoskey** to try to get out of the harbor. The steamer made the attempt but became trapped in ice between the piers and was unable to move, either forward into the lake or back to the dock.

Meanwhile at Saugatuck, 39 miles north of St. Joseph and 14 miles north of South Haven, the weather finally was clear enough to inspect the wreckage which had been discovered Sunday. The weekly *Saugatuck Commercial* for February 1 reported:

Last Sunday it was discovered that a quantity of wreckage from the lost steamer **Chicora** was imbedded in ice off this place, but owing to the inclement weather no extended search could be made that day.

The next day a party of a dozen or more from this village went out on the lake at a point opposite Capt. Reid's residence and at a distance of about three quarters of a mile from shore found a line of wreckage strewn in the ice in a line parallel with the shore and reaching probably from this harbor as far south as South Haven, where wreckage from the boat was first discovered. A portion of the hurricane deck of the steamer was found standing edgewise in the ice with a portion at least eight feet square exposed. Both spars of the boat were found they being less than a half mile apart. Both were broken off. One gang plank was found and the oars from her life boats.

It is evident that before her upper works came ashore they were well broken up by the sea and ice and it all tends to support the theory that the boat foundered about mid-lake. With the exception of the spars nothing has been discovered that came from below the promenade deck.

A telegram was sent to Benton Harbor by D. L. Barber, a Saugatuck shop keeper and father-in-law of W. J. Hancock. It read:

> FOUND HER TWO MASTS. MAIN MAST CHOPPED OFF AT MAIN DECK; FORWARD MAST BROKEN OFF AT MAIN DECK. MOST OF CABIN STREWN ALONG THE SHORE.

It became a matter of some heated discussion whether the main mast had been broken off or chopped off. Ship captain and builder R. C. Brittain of Saugatuck was adamant. In a letter to Graham dated January 28 he wrote:

> I sent a man out on the ice about 1 1/2 miles and 2 miles south of this place to examine some wreckage. They found both of her spars -- the foremost one broken off at the main deck and the mainmast cut off at the main deck. He is positive and you may rely on what he says. He says the axe marks are plain and he is not mistaken. The length of the mast cut off is 21 paces or about 50 feet from rigging band to saddle, and from saddle to where cut off 6 1/2 paces, or about 20 feet. The mast is about 16 inches in diameter at the butt. Will send some more men out tomorrow and report anything of importance.

However, later when the masts had actually been hauled to shore and could be examined closely the *Palladium* reporter wrote that on closer examination the marks were not conclusive:

THE MARINER'S FOE.

The King of the Icy Inland Seas is on His Throne.
An editorial cartoon from the January 26 Detroit Journal.

[The main mast] was not chopped away, it was discovered after careful examination, but had been broken off at or near the main deck, just below where it rested in the stoops. This portion of the mast was in fairly good condition. The foremast showed marks of a hard struggle with the elements. It had evidently been broken off near the hurricane deck before the upper works were swept away, and, being held to the hulk by guy ropes, battered the laboring boat until it was torn away.

The matter was considered important because a chopped mast would indicate that the boat had not foundered quickly, but stayed afloat long enough for the crew to try to save it and themselves.

The *Allegan Gazette* reported:

> At first it was reported that the foremast was broken and the mainmast cut, but closer investigation found both to have been broken. Only one barrel of flour has yet been seen and this, with the fact that none of the boat's timbers have been found causes faint hope that the hull may yet be afloat, and, if so, bearing alive some of the crew. On this account memorial services which had been arranged have been postponed. The supposed cutting of the mainmast was presumed to indicate a long struggle with the failing vessel.

This was the only report anywhere that memorial services had been delayed and is probably untrue. In fact the *Palladium* published on Monday a letter from E. F. Strickland, a former resident of the area, noting, "I feel an almost personal loss, as if a link between home and this great heartless wilderness of a city has been broken, as indeed it has." He suggested that memorial services be made a union service, "all distinctions of creed and church should be forgotten and all united in services in memory of the brave craft, commander and crew, that belong to our whole people, and are held in sorrowful remembrance by us all." Plans were set in motion for this to be done in Benton Harbor.

Clerk W. J. Hancock, who resided at Saugatuck, took the train north and arrived home Monday afternoon. The *Grand Rapids Democrat* reported:

> He also saw the wreckage and has made all arrangements to go out in the morning with a selected crew to search the lake for additional tidings of the ill-fated vessel. Mr. Hancock now believes that she foundered nearly twenty miles further north than was at first supposed. . . . Searching will be commenced at daylight in the morning by many people and the beach and water for miles will be patrolled.

10

The Dickinson Tries

Tuesday, January 29

On Tuesday Graham telegraphed the Independent Towing Company of Chicago, asking that they send out a tug and a telegram was received stating that the tug **William Dickinson** had left Chicago for St. Joseph and was expected to arrive at the ice field opposite the harbor by 5 p.m. The plan announced at Benton Harbor was for the captain of the **Dickinson** to assist in breaking out the **Petoskey** and, if the weather held favorable, for both the **Dickinson** and **Petoskey** to go north to South Haven and make a thorough search. Graham was especially pleased to get the **Dickinson**. She was one of the largest tugs in Chicago, 88 feet in length, 19.5 feet in breadth and drawing 12 1/2 feet of water. She had two engines and boilers built to generate 140 pounds of steam. Her propeller was 9 feet in diameter. In addition she was a home town boat, having been built by E. W. Heath of Benton Harbor.

Captain Thomas Barry was in charge of the tug. Crew members included Captain Jonathan McAvoy, first mate and assistant wheelsman; Frank Varney (another report says Bonney), engineer; Sidney Pierson, fireman; James McCormick, fireman; and Lawrence Ricks, steward. In addition "a number of press representatives and artists" were aboard. When the **Dickinson** left Chicago she had 32 tons of coal on board, dynamite to blast a path through the ice and food enough to last the crew for several weeks.

Captain Barry was interviewed by a *Chicago InterOcean* reporter before his departure:

> "Our instructions," said Captain Barry, helping the provender into the galley, "are to make due for Benton Harbor. We are not to make a search for the **Chicora**, but go to break up enough of the ice at the end of the pier at Benton Harbor to release the **Petoskey**. Of course, we will keep our eyes open for her on the way up and if we run across her we will take a long chance at discipline for disobeying orders. With any kind of luck and no delays we will get to Benton Harbor before sundown. The sea is a bit high and the wind a bit strong, but if we don't ride both it will be because the staunchest craft in these parts is unequal to it."

Crowds lined the bluffs at St. Joseph to watch for the **Dickinson**. When she failed to arrive before dark the St. Joseph lighthouse keeper and the *Chicago Inter-Ocean* reporter at Benton Harbor crossed the river on the ice and climbed the lighthouse tower to a height of about 50 feet above the lake, but could see nothing but great mountains of ice in the strong night glass.

*The tug **William Dickinson** from a January 30 InterOcean.*

The **Petoskey**, which was still stuck in the ice between the piers, spent most of Tuesday blowing her whistle at intervals to help the **Dickinson** find the harbor. It was not until a wire was received on Wednesday morning that Graham learned that the tug had returned to Chicago and its owners were uncertain when it would be possible to get out.

According to a later story in the *Chicago Herald*:

> Captain Barry and five other brave men faced a fierce northwest wind yesterday morning and started out to find the wrecked **Chicora** and the twenty-four poor mortals who died in the hurricane. They had the tug **Dickinson** loaded heavy with coal and provisions and armed for a hard battle with ice and waves, they opened all the valves and piled high the fire pans of the little giant and waved a farewell to the friends who formed a line along the dock at the end of Franklin street. There was no open sea within range of the glass and the hard winds of a few days ago had piled the floes into hills and drifts. His course was straight across the lake into the harbor at St. Joseph. The **Petoskey** was to join him there and the two were to patrol the east coast in company.
>
> The plan was all changed early in the afternoon. Captain Barry, when some twenty miles out, concluded it was not wise to proceed. The powerful **Dickinson** was banked to fight every inch of the way. So he turned back and reached port in safety.

Meanwhile back in Saugatuck the weather had cleared a little and the search was on. The *Benton Harbor Daily Palladium* reported:

> Into the mass a party of 100 explorers for wreckage of the **Chicora** plunged at daybreak this morning and proceeded to a point

nearly two miles from shore. Here they were detailed into parties. One . . . went south; another . . . went north; and the third, with the life boat of the United States Life Saving station, stayed at the discharging point under Shipbuilder Dunham [probably Charles Durham who built boats for R. C. Brittain] to go to the relief of either of the other parties. Clerk Hancock of the **Chicora** was with the south-bound party. Wreckage was found at intervals in the ice. Some of it was firmly imbedded and so large that the removal was impossible. One mass from the forward bulwarks is ten by twelve feet square and stands upright. Both foremast and mainmast were found near together.

One of the most telling pieces was the passenger gang-plank that was discovered imbedded in the ice four miles south of the port, two miles off shore. It was chopped out of the ice and was intact. No marks of violence were on it to indicate that it had passed through an awful storm, but telltale spots of red told a story that no amount of splintering of the plank would. In case of danger the gang plank of a vessel is one of the first things a sailor looks to for safety. It is a life raft to him. In the terrible struggle of the boat against the sea with the odds against the boat, the gang-plank is kept in sight. In that unequal fight when the upper works were being shattered and members of the crew received injury, the plank would be the safety buoy to which they would turn and lash themselves. There is no evidence that anyone was lashed to it, but those red spots indicate that it was clasped in the arms of those whose lives were endangered and that it was looked to as a protector.

The party exploring northward proceeded five miles and in that distance found a barrel of flour, the lintel of the door of the captain's cabin with the word "Captain" lettered thereon, and a silver fifty-cent piece fixed in a crack of a state room door. This lintel will be sent to Mrs. Stines. Although Mr. Hancock says no vessels will join in the search until the storms abate, exploring parties will traverse the ice to South Haven. They will go out at daybreak in the morning. It is now definitely known that no wreckage lies beyond five miles north of this point. Therefore the limit of wreckage are Saugatuck on the north and South Haven on the south. Clerk Hancock is now convinced that the **Chicora** was lost while heading for the west shore after she was overtaken by the storm.

The next issue of the *Palladium* reported that the dark red stains on the gangplank were paint "and had been noticed many times by the employees around the boat dock. The ship carpenter remembers when the paint was dropped on the plank."

11

Petoskey Freed for the Moment

Wednesday, January 30

Some Chicago papers reported that the tug **Dickinson** was steeled to make another attempt at getting out onto Lake Michigan, but the *Palladium* indicated that no word of that possibility had been received in Benton Harbor.

A long dispatch from Saugatuck describes the search for wreckage and bodies:

> Hundreds of persons are searching the frozen lake for wreckage between Saugatuck and South Haven. Several exploring parties from here searched the ice off this shore for a distance of several miles today and the only find of importance was that of a board upon which the name "**Chicora**" is painted in gold. It was from the after part of the cabin. The name was found by two young men of this village who turned it over to Clark W. J. Hancock, who will forward it to Capt. Graham at Benton Harbor.
>
> The passenger gang plank was not brought ashore to-day, and it is doubtful if any body of its size and weight can be pulled to land over such fields of irregular ice. The foremast was brought in by twenty men with ropes at a point three miles south of here.
>
> A staff correspondent of *The Democrat* made a trip lakeward with a party of Saugatuck men today. The distance traversed was three miles from shore. At that distance open water could not be seen by aid of glasses. Excepting a brief interval snow fell during the entire time the explorers were out. For a few minutes during the afternoon, however, the clouds parted and the sun shone brightly on the ice fields. The atmosphere during this brief interval was quite clear, the water could be seen, and with powerful glasses an area of fifteen miles north and south could be covered with sufficient accuracy to determine that no larger piece of wreckage than those already mentioned in these dispatches and surely no parts of the hull were within range. Near the point where a section of the bulwarks is imprisoned by the dense ice may be found richly finished woodwork from the cabin. The deduction is therefore reasonable that all of the vessel's upper works went overboard at nearly the same time. The ice fields extend lakeward from four to six miles at various points and along the entire shore from many miles north down nearly or quite to the Indiana line. It is a vast field of gorged ice, pressed, massed and frozen together so irregularly as to render passage through or over it extremely hazardous, as well as extremely laborious. . . .

STEAMER PETOSKEY FAST IN AN ICE FIELD.

It is evident, therefore, that so long as the ice remains as it is, and retains its present heavy covering of snow, any important discovery is mere accident. It is useless, therefore, in the face of prevailing conditions, for vessels to undertake to search for either the bodies of the crew or the hull of the vessel. It is equally useless for any vessel to attempt to enter these fields. Nothing could be accomplished. The inactivity of the Graham & Morton people in the matter of a thorough systematic search has been criticized by press and public, but one who surveys these fields will see how little may be gained by it.

So soon as wind or weather shall scatter the ice and snow and permit an effective search such will be vigorously prosecuted, but that time is not now.

On the St. Joseph River the steamer **Petoskey** was finally loosed from the ice packed at the mouth of the harbor and backed down to the Vandalia docks. The *Chicago InterOcean* described how the release was accomplished:

> A large crowd of men early this morning sawed into the ice to the south of the **Petoskey** and between the steamer and the south pier. Great blocks had been sawed out and drawn into open water by means of poles and ropes. By noon a large strip had been disposed of, and hundreds of anxious eyes watched for the hour that might bid the **Petoskey** move from her perilous position.
>
> The tug **Tramp**, which had been lying at her dock down the river, got up a full head of steam and was soon pushing her steel-clad prow through the resisting heavy ice on the river in the direction of the **Petoskey** at the end of the piers. The **Tramp** followed in the wake of the large steamer, and the great blocks of ice which had been thrown in almost every way by the **Petoskey** and which were soon a frozen mass of jagged icebergs were thrown down and cast aside before the mighty pressure of the little tug. The **Tramp** soon arrived at the vessel's side and the **Petoskey** was soon released and proudly escorted down the river to her docks by the faithful workmen and the rescuing tug.

Despite the wreckage and the continuing cold temperatures and wind, hope continued to be held that all was not yet lost. A newspaper account filed Wednesday by a reporter of the *Chicago InterOcean* from St. Joseph and printed January 31 stated, "Belief that the hull of the steamer **Chicora** is still afloat and that sooner or later she will be found is daily strengthening here. That all aboard her when she started on her fatal cruise are alive is not entertained even as a last hope, though it is believed that some are and will yet reach shore."

In the January 30 issue of the *Detroit Free Press* Mrs. C. D. Simons, wife of the first mate who resided in Detroit, was quoted as remarking, "Mr. Simons will be back again. The boat still floats."

12

A Brother is Ready to Sail

Thursday, January 31

Finally on January 31 Graham received a telegram from Milwaukee that the steamer **City of Ludington** of the Goodrich Line, commanded by Captain Henry Stines, a brother of the **Chicora's** captain, would travel across the lake approaching the Michigan shore somewhere north of Saugatuck then turn southward and cruise slowly along the outer edge of the ice fields to St. Joseph. The **Ludington** had authorization from her owners to stay out on the search as long as the captain deemed it advisable. Captain Henry Stines had worked for Goodrich several years and in the summer served as captain of the **Virginia**.

A second telegram which arrived at 3 p.m. in the afternoon was from W. W. Bromley, the Milwaukee Graham & Morton agent, and stated that the **Ludington** was taking on a big supply of coal and would get away during the afternoon. The wire added that G. S. Whistler, general passenger agent for Graham & Morton in Chicago, was aboard the steamer and would wire any news from all available points. In addition a set of signals was prearranged. An American flag would be run out on the foremast if any of the crew had been found living; signal from the gaff if found dead; from aft if hull only was found.

A third telegram at 3:30 relayed the information that the **Ludington** had just left Milwaukee.

In addition to the regular crew of the **City of Ludington**, the crew of the steamer **Racine** boarded the **Ludington** at Milwaukee with the plan that they would ride her full circle from Milwaukee around the lake and back to Manitowoc. All aboard were on watch constantly, and the plan was to cover a sweep of 24 miles from the shore of Michigan far out into the lake on both sides of the **Ludington**. Also on board were all of the powerful glasses they could find to give them as much range as possible.

The **City of Ludington** was a steam propeller of 842 gross tons, 738 net tons, just under 180 feet in length with a beam of 35.4 feet. She had been built in Manitowoc, Wisconsin, by Rand and Burger in 1880 specifically for the cross lake package freight and passenger traffic, originally between Ludington and Milwaukee, but later she worked on other routes. To strengthen her for winter use she was given a heavily reinforced bow and a sturdy stiff hull. Arched trusses were added for additional longitudinal strength to her hull. Because of her strength and power she was often used to assist other boats which ran into difficulties during winter navigation. She was also the first Goodrich steamer equipped with an electric searchlight.

According to a detailed account written later by G. S. Whistler:

> The **Ludington** struck the slush ice off Grand Haven at about
> 11 o'clock Thursday night. There was a gale blowing at the time and

the sea was rolling high. Capt. Stines was on duty all the way over and ran the **Ludington** about three boat lengths into the ice. This was not far enough to secure it from the action of the high sea and it pounded heavily on the ice all night. We were within sight of the Grand Haven light, the boat was pounding on the ice so hard that I urged Capt. Stines to run farther into the ice so that we could get away from the action of the sea, but he said he was determined to search for the **Chicora** on the following morning and he was afraid if he ran farther into the ice his boat might become fast. The temperature was 20 degrees below zero, but notwithstanding this the Captain remained on duty all night.

*Goodrich Transit company's **City of Ludington***

In Chicago, J. W. Yakes had a vision in which he saw the hull of the **Chicora** fast in the ice two and one-half miles north and east of Muskegon. In his vision, however, he did not see whether any of the crew were alive.

In many of the city papers news of the **Chicora** was pushed inside and replaced on the front page by wire dispatches announcing the sinking of the German steamer **Elbe** which had collided with the **Craithie** on Wednesday, January 30, in the North Sea en route to New York from Southampton, England. More than 300 lives were lost.

13

The Ludington Searches the Coast

Friday, February 1

After a sleepless night while his vessel was pounded by the waves Captain Stines, in command of the **City of Ludington,** was ready for the search. Agent Whistler continues his narrative:

> At 7 o'clock Friday morning the **Ludington** started on the search. As soon as it started south from Grand Haven Capt. Stines went on the bridge of the boat, and despite the low temperature and the howling gale he remained in that exposed position from that time until late in the afternoon, never once leaving it even to eat. He was so determined that the search should be thorough and that nothing in the eighty miles of lake which we searched should escape his notice that he would not trust the work to any one else.
>
> All day the boat kept along the outer edge of the ice pack, which at some points extended ten or twelve miles from the shore and which narrowed down to three and a half or four miles near St. Joe. All of this ice was scanned carefully, but not a particle of wreckage could be discovered. Outside of the old ice about a mile and a half of new ice had formed. This is separated from the old ice by a windrow about five feet high.

Crowds of people braced against the cold wind lined the bluff at St. Joseph. The steamer **City of Ludington** came into sight about 3 p.m. showing no signal of any kind. When she neared the harbor entrance there was a noticeable pause and change of direction, Agent Whistler later said that they had seen "a black speck in the ice and though it might be some of the wreckage. We put in towards the harbor, but it proved to be black snow." Then Capt. Stines ordered the boat back. She did not attempt to enter the harbor, still blocked by three miles of ice with a solid outer wall 15 to 20 feet thick, but turned and headed south, apparently for Chicago.

Graham waited expecting to receive a telegram when the **Ludington** reached Chicago, but received no news from the vessel on Friday.

Finally the following afternoon at 1 p.m. word was received from Sheboygan, Wisconsin. Agent Whistler reported that the boat had held to the Chicago course until well over toward the west shore but did not enter the city. At the Grosse Point light, north of Chicago the **Ludington** turned northward and steamed slowly to Sheboygan "to make the circuit complete, in the hope that something might be discovered that would throw additional light on the **Chicora** disaster." Whistler said, "Captain Stines was on the deck constantly from the time we left Milwaukee until we arrived in

Sheboygan. He is much chagrined at the result of his search, but is convinced of the utter futility of any further efforts to find the **Chicora**. It will be useless to send out tugs as they cannot find anything and cannot do anything in that ice."

The St. Joseph newspaper reported that the Ludington arrived in Sheboygan after a 48 hour, 300 mile trip "having had a hard uncomfortable, profitless voyage and covered with tons of ice until she resembled an arctic vessel."

*Citizens gathered in the park along the bluff St. Joseph to watch for a signal from the **City of Ludington**. This postcard from about 1900 shows a steam boat far out into Lake Michigan at right. An amusement park was constructed on the lake shore below the bluff in 1880 and remained in business until 1970.*

14

Captain Robertson's Story

Saturday, February 2

By Saturday at least the sky was looking a little brighter. According to the *Palladium* "Since the weather has become more settled, the ice shows signs of breaking up and patches of water are appearing here and there in the field, while some of the loose ice along the outer edge has floated away. Mr. Graham telegraphed his agent in Chicago this morning to send tugs over to this side as soon as possible to break a channel into the harbor so that the **Petoskey** can be got out."

The *St. Joseph Saturday Herald* commented, "As soon as they can break through the huge wall of ice that now blocks the harbor the **Petoskey** and **Tramp** will go on a search down the lake in the hope that they may find something that will help to clear up a part, at least, of the mystery that surrounds the last trip of the **Chicora**. The bereaved families are bearing up bravely under their great affliction."

In preparation the **Petoskey** moved over to the Big Four dock to take on a partial load of freight "so as to be in better shape to assist in breaking the ice."

With little other hard news to occupy its columns the *Benton Harbor Daily Palladium* attempted to deal with another of what it called "fake" stories that had been published in the *Grand Rapids Democrat* which picked it up from the Manistee papers which apparently got it first from the *Evening Wisconsin* of Milwaukee.

The story was recounted in the February 1, 1895, issue of the *Manistee Advocate* with corroboration from the captain himself:

Why the Petoskey Remained in Port on Monday

One fact in connection with the loss of the steamer **Chicora** which is being talked about among vessel masters but has not become generally known is that Capt. Robertson early last Monday morning, or on the day of the disaster, tendered a peremptory resignation of the command of the steamer **Petoskey**, which is under charter to the Graham & Morton Transportation company and was then lying at St. Joseph, having arrived from Milwaukee on the day previous. Capt. Robertson notified P. J. Klein of the Northern Michigan line of his action, and Mr. Klein also received similar information by telegraph from J. H. Graham of the Graham & Morton line. Beyond replying to Mr. Morton [the writer meant Graham] that the management of the **Petoskey** was in his hands Mr. Klein paid no attention to the matter, and it is understood that Capt. John Griffin of the steamer **R. C. Reid** was appointed to fill the vacancy. Current report has it that

Capt. Robertson's unexpected action was based upon an order to return to Milwaukee at once, when existing weather conditions and barometric indications warned him not to venture out. If these are the facts in the case Capt. Robertson deserves commendation for his course, as it shows him to be a seaman possessed of prudence and good judgment -- *Evening Wisconsin*

Capt. Robertson called on us Tuesday and verified the above statements, by reiterating that he received orders from Graham & Morton to go out at 7 o'clock, Monday, January 2 [sic], but refused to go, and Capt. John Griffin was placed at the helm.

The *Manistee Daily News* which carried a similar story in the January 30 edition under the headline "He Refused to Go," added the information that after Captain Griffin had been placed in charge, and before the **Petoskey** could be gotten ready, "telegrams began to come in and she did not leave her dock. . . The foresight and judgment of Captain Robinson undoubtedly saved the **Petoskey** from the **Chicora's** fate."

The *Benton Harbor Daily Palladium* for February 2 branded the entire incident false. "The facts are Capt. Robinson was not at that time captain of the **Petoskey**, but was removed for cause (was heard to say it was the first time he had ever been discharged) some days previous to Jan. 21; and furthermore Mr. Graham gave the crew of the **Petoskey** orders not to leave port that day for the reason that a severe storm was threatened."

All of the newspaper accounts that mention a captain on the **Petoskey** during the period immediately following the loss of the **Chicora** name John Griffin without further explanation. His usual command, the **R. C. Reid**, was in dry dock so he was available for duty and it is likely that Graham preferred one of his own men to the sometimes irascible Captain Robertson. The last paragraph of the *Manistee Advocate* story which dates the refusal to sail in bad weather and subsequent replacement as an incident that happened on January 2, may be more than a typographical error. It may be that Captain Robertson was using an earlier incident to discredit Graham & Morton because he was angry with them.

The **Petoskey's** enrollment papers do not reflect the change in master. The official enrollment issued May 29, 1894, at Chicago lists the owner as "E. W. Seymour of Chicago, Ill., Acting Secretary of the Northern Michigan Transportation Company" and names Captain W. P. Robertson as Master. Although a change of masters did not require a new enrollment, attachments noting the change were usually glued or otherwise attached to the official certificates. This should have been done even though the vessel was under charter, and not owned by Graham & Morton.

Captain Robertson returned to Manistee. Near the end of February he was named captain of the ferry boat **Toledo & Ann Arbor No. 2** while the vessel was frozen fast in the ice near Manistee. In the spring when the charter to Graham & Morton was up, he returned to his old job on the **Petoskey**. Although the captain's name is spelled Robertson on the documents for the **Petoskey**, in newspaper columns he is called Robinson nearly as often as Robertson. To add to the confusion in mid-December 1895, he was married to Grace E. Robinson of Muskegon.

15

"Is It the Chicora?"

Sunday, February 3

On Sunday afternoon the twin cities of Benton Harbor and St. Joseph were beginning to settle down after the events of the previous two weeks. Into this calm a message arrived at the telegraph office addressed to E. E. Rouse, a reporter for the *Chicago Record*, from the editors of his newspaper. It read:

> HULL OF VESSEL BELIEVED TO BE CHICORA IN SIGHT OFF SOUTH CHICAGO, WITH FOURTEEN MEN OR MORE ON BOARD. WIRE EFFECT OF NEWS IN BENTON HARBOR AND OTHER CITIES.

Rouse hunted up Graham who immediately wired the Western Union office in South Chicago for more information. The word spread through St. Joseph and Benton Harbor rapidly and churches and houses emptied as crowds gathered at the telegraph office and at the Graham & Morton offices. Memorial services that were to take place on Sunday afternoon were canceled and impromptu thanksgiving services took their places.

Telegrams followed in quick succession. One received at Benton Harbor at 3:10 p.m., from South Chicago office manager J. F. Pierson, stated:

> A VESSEL SIGHTED OFF ABOUT SEVEN MILES, SUPPOSED TO BE THE CHICORA. SIGNALS NINE ALIVE.

At 4:30 p.m. Pierson wired:

> TUGS CANNOT GET OUT FROM HERE. ICE A MILE WIDE. TWO TUGS SENT FROM CHICAGO. RELIEF PARTY GONE TO WHITING AND MILLERS, INDIANA. EVERYTHING THAT CAN BE DONE IS BEING DONE.

And 20 minutes later another telegram was received from South Chicago. This one was signed by "Chief Fire Department."

> CRIB KEEPERS DID NOT SEE ANY BOAT LAST NIGHT BUT THERE IS A BOAT NOW FLOATING OFF SOUTH CHICAGO WHICH IS WITHOUT DOUBT THE CHICORA, AS HER NAME CAN BE READ THROUGH A FIELD GLASS FROM SHORE. TWO TUGS GONE TO ASSISTANCE.

The first reaction of Graham was to discredit the news. He speculated to callers that the hull at Chicago was probably a sailboat fast in the ice. But the telegram stating that the name could be read through field glasses dispelled every doubt and cheers rose from the crowd.

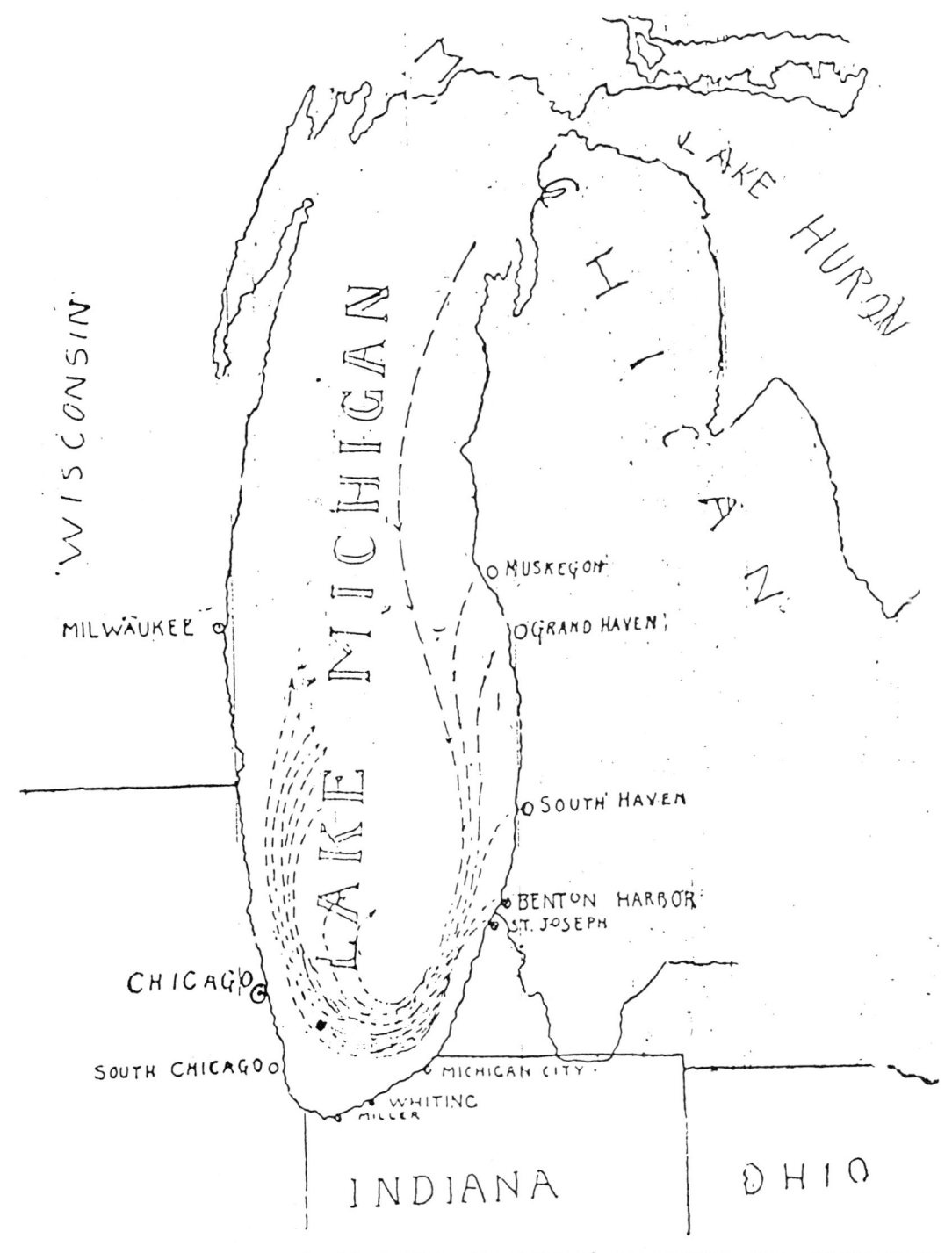

WEATHER BUREAU MAP OF LAKE MICHIGAN SHOWING ITS CURRENTS.

*A map offered by a Chicago newspaper to explain why it was plausible that the hull of the **Chicora** might drift toward South Chicago.*

Even while he was waiting for more information Graham began to make arrangements for a special train to carry rescuers and others from the twin cities to Whiting, the nearest port to the object. He wired General Superintendent J. K. V. Agnew of the Chicago and West Michigan Railway for a train of three coaches to arrive in the Chicago area at midnight. The local agent for the Big Four and Lake Shore railroads set in motion plans for a similar train.

The *Palladium* put out an extra edition at 5 p.m. using the same news as the previous edition except on the local page. There they repeated, verbatim the telegrams given above under the hopeful, but guarded headline:

IS IT THE CHICORA?

**More News Awaited Here
with Breathless Interest**

And at the end of the headlines and telegrams added the following disclaimer to the report:

> We give the above particulars for what they are worth. No other details have been received here and we dare not venture an opinion.
> Mr. Graham does not believe the **Chicora's** hull has been sighted. He is using the telegraph freely to ascertain more particulars.
> The community is in a feverish state of excitement and inquiry.
> The sighted hull may belong to some other vessel.
> The whole story may be pure rumor or imagination. We can only wait for particulars.

Although others would later claim to have spotted it earlier, the Chicago newspapers in trying to piece together the story the following day, place the first sighting of the object that was acted upon to the men of Fire Engine Co. No. 74. They were returning to the station Sunday morning at about 10 a.m., after being out most of the night fighting a fire that consumed one entire business block in downtown South Chicago. As they were crossing 98th Street they saw an object out in the lake which, the *Tribune* later said, "in their eyes did not have the appearance of an iceberg."

The matter was reported to Marshal Smith who took the strongest glasses he could find out to the lighthouse pier at the mouth of the Calumet River. The newspaper reported the following day:

> With his glass Marshal Smith made out an object that looked to him like the dismantled hull of a vessel. It appeared to be wedged in an ice flow that was all of five miles long. It seemed to be covered with ice, but the back part of it, round like the stern of a vessel, showed black and was clear of ice.
> Marshal Smith went back to his station and ordered the fire boat **Chicago** and all of the tugs in the Calumet River out to the

relief of what he concluded was the wreck of the **Chicora**. Besides the fire boat there lay in the river the tugs **Halliday, Hausler,** and **Alphic** [probably the **C. W. Elphicke**], but none of them could break through the thick ice on the river except perhaps the **Hausler.**

Of course the news that the wreck of the **Chicora** was off South Chicago stirred enormous excitement in the iron-making suburb. All the people flocked to the lakeshore. Every telescope and binocular in the town was brought out...

Some observers were sure they saw men aboard the hulk. They could see them moving their hats. They could see them leaving the wreck and taking to the ice-flow. Some counted fifteen men and some counted nineteen. It was reported that the crew were making their way shorewards...

DARK OBJECT OFF SOUTH CHICAGO THOUGHT TO BE THE HULL OF THE WRECKED CHICORA.

John Wright, the engineer of the tug **M. Hausler** of South Chicago, watched the object with a pair of field glasses and was unconvinced but could understand the conviction of the less experienced. He was quoted in a Monday *Chicago Tribune* story:

> I am certain the object was not the hull of a vessel. I often have noticed the strange effect which a dark object will have upon a field of white ice. We have run miles with a tug after an object which looked like a boat only to find it was a cake of dirty ice, which had

been thrown up by the action of the sea. Not long ago we had a hard chase after a supposed wreck. Every man on the tug was confident it was the hull and broken upperworks of a steamer. When we caught up to it we found a fence had been carried out in the lake by an ice floe.

I am not surprised that people on shore today thought they saw the black hull of the **Chicora**. Much of the time the object was so indistinct that the men looking at it could imagine most everything. If I had not had so many years' experience running out on the lake from South Chicago, probably I would have been of the opinion, that the object was really the hull of a vessel.

Keeper of the lighthouse at the mouth of the Calumet river, A. J. Davenport, watched the object for more than an hour and always doubted that it was a hull. He told am *InterOcean* reporter:

I saw nothing to settled the question definitely whether a floating wreck went past or not. When I saw it first it was about three miles out and was very low down in the water, and that is one reason why I have doubts about its being a wrecked vessel. It was a long, black object in the ice, and was about the length of the hull of a vessel like the **Chicora**, but I could not see its form distinctly. At this time of the year when the lake is filled with ice it often happens that a mass of dirty and blackened snow floats by on an ice flow. Sometimes snow which is taken from the streets of the city and dumped into the river floats away into the lake, and on account of its darkened color it can be seen in the lake for many miles. What I saw today may have been the hull of a vessel, but for anything I could make out it might just as easily have been a mass of this blackened snow floating in the ice.

Andrew Crawford was driving in Lincoln Park when one of his sons rushed bareheaded from the house to find and catch up with the carriage. Crawford drove at once to the offices of the company and stayed there into the night. He was visited in the afternoon by Mrs. Morris, the sister of Captain Stines, who arrived according to the *Chicago Tribune* "almost fainting and out of breath. She told Mr. Crawford the Captain's old mother was being torn between hope and anxiety and Mrs. Morris tearfully begged some one to give her definite information."

Crawford was the biggest skeptic. The *Chicago Tribune* later wrote, "The conflicting reports raised him one moment to the pinnacle of absolute confidence. Then someone could telephone that the whole story was a canard and Mr. Crawford's head would sink thoughtfully upon his breast. Once when a wild rumor came to him over the telephone that eighteen men had actually been taken from the hull of the missing boat the usually reserved and dignified millionaire jumped from his chair and shook hands enthusiastically with every one in the room. In a short time, however, the telegram was proven to be without basis and the old atmosphere of gloom regained its sway."

THE RESCUE TRAIN LEAVING SOUTH CHICAGO FOR WHITING AND MILLER.

Captain W. H. Jenkins, of the Fifteenth Precinct police station, sent the patrol wagon along the beach. What they found was described the next day in the *Daily Calumet*:

> No movement could be seen on the floating object which turned round and round as it was driven by the current and the wind. One moment it could hardly be distinguished, and then it would swing slowly around until a long, black line was exposed to view, like the broadside of a steamer. This would again turn round until only a faint, dark speck could be seen across the intervening space of ice floes and water.

The object continued to drift southward. By 2 p.m. observers at South Chicago could barely make it out. It was calculated from the direction of the wind and the movement of the floe that it would drift near Whiting, Indiana, six miles from South Chicago and three miles over the Indiana line. Master Mechanic McDermott of the Baltimore and Ohio railroad got out a switch engine to follow along the lake shore or the tracks of that road. Police Captain Jenkins and Sgt. McNamara, Station Agent J L. Davis of the B & O and Ernest Hummel of South Chicago were taken aboard.

The *Chicago Tribune* describes the trip:

> The engine started from the railroad yards at 3 o'clock. On the siding in the suburbs of South Chicago the Baltimore and Ohio wrecking train was found with its crew aboard. McDermott stopped the engine, coupled the engine to the wrecking train and started again to Whiting, where it was believed the ship-wrecked men were lodged in the ice awaiting the coming of help. The engine was put to the limit of its speed and arrived at Whiting in a few minutes.
> Rumors of the **Chicora** were flying thickly there. It was said by those at Whiting with whom the rescuing party talked that the

Chicora had been sighted lying off the shore opposite Miller's. The track was clear, and without a moment's delay, the wrecking train started to Miller's. The throttle of the engine was pulled wide open. The hope of saving life made the moments precious.

When they arrived at Miller's the reports received there were rather vague. The railroad station is a mile and a half from the lake shore at this point. They hastened to the shore, but nothing could be seen there. A number of persons were scattered along the lake shore and others had gone as far out on the ice as they dared, but no one had seen anything there to indicate that the lost **Chicora** was anywhere near. They had brought along with them block and tackles and other apparatus from the wrecking train which might be used to render assistance were there an occasion for it.

The party returned to the train and started back for South Chicago. At Whiting they stopped again and this time they were told that two tugs were lying off that point about four miles from shore and working around the wreck of the **Chicora**. It was nearly sunset and through the thick weather and the snow nothing could be seen from shore. They waited a while and the whistle of tugs could be heard out on the lake. After waiting long enough to assure themselves that they could do nothing in the way of rendering help the rescuing party and their special train returned to South Chicago.

A second extra edition of the *Benton Harbor Palladium* at 7 p.m. used the same words in the headline as the first edition, but two words were transposed in the top line and the punctuation on the end of the sentence was changed.

IT IS THE CHICORA!

All of the subheadlines were the same. The body of the report was the same as that contained in the 5 p.m. edition with the following telegrams added to the end of the account:

Chicago, Feb. 3, 6:30 p.m.
CHICORA SIGHTED AT SOUTH CHICAGO. TEN TUGS WORKING. PEOPLE SEEN ABOARD. SHE IS DRIFTING SOUTHEAST. THE LIFE SAVING CREW LEFT ON A SPECIAL TRAIN TO MEET THE CHICORA AT MICHIGAN CITY.
SO. CHICAGO POLICE DEP'T

Chicago via Wabash, Feb. 3
CHICORA ASHORE NEAR WHITING, IND., AND A TUG HAS GONE AFTER THE MEN. NINETEEN HAVE BEEN SIGHTED ON HER. THEY EXPECT TO GET THEM OFF BY MORNING.

So. Chicago, Feb. 3, 7:30 p.m.
HAVE JUST RETURNED FROM WHITING, IND. PARTIES THERE REPORT SEEING WRECK AT 4'O CLOCK, WITH TUG WORKING TO GET TO IT. AT 6:30 TUG WAS STILL THERE. AS IT IS SNOWING WE THINK THEY MUST HAVE FOUND THE BOAT TO KEEP THEM OUT AFTER DARK.
H. F. HEATH

Niles, Feb. 3, 8 p.m.
TO MAYOR FIFIELD, BENTON HARBOR:
  NILES REJOICES WITH YOU FOR THE NEWS, **CHICORA** FOUND AND ALL SAFE.
  E. F. WOODCOCK, MAYOR OF NILES

The *Chicago Tribune* wrote the next day, "News was received with wildest enthusiasm at St. Joseph. Hundreds wept for joy, yet feared the news too good to be true. Special trains will be sent out from Grand Rapids to convey several hundred Benton Harbor and St. Joseph people to meet the men as soon as they are rescued. Arrangements are being made for public rejoicing, ringing of bells, blowing of whistles of factories, shops and all steam vessels; bonfires are being made, and people are using every means to show their joy. Old men, cramped with rheumatism were seen to run like young boys, forgetting their aches. Mr. Graham's face evinces great happiness as if he himself had been rescued from death."

In Chicago when news reached the city about the sighting of something, possibly the **Chicora**, off South Chicago word was sent to the Vessel Owners' Towing company asking for two tugs to investigate the situation and tender aid if possible. In response the tug **Protection** was ordered into immediate service. A fire was started under her boilers and she left the harbor at 2 p.m., followed an hour later by the **Calumet**.

The conditions were not favorable for a thorough search. A heavy ice covering the lake made progress slow, the wind was carrying the object out of sight of the watchers on shore, and it was beginning to get dark. An evening snow storm soon after the vessel left port added to the problems.

The **Protection** was manned by Capt. Henry Consaul, Engineer George McLean with Michael Fenton, also an engineer, as volunteer fireman, and Jack Hogarth, deck hand. Captain Frank Miner was in command of the **Calumet**, his crew consisted of John Runyan, mate; E. Higgins, engineer; L. French, fireman.

The *Chicago Tribune* describes the search:

> When the **Protection** arrived off South Chicago nothing could be seen of the object of its search, so the Captain put into the mouth of the Calumet River and went in search of a telephone to get reports from further down the shore. From Whiting and other points he received information that what appeared to be the ice-covered hulk of a large vessel was slowly drifting southward. Capt. Consaul decided to go further south and see what the object was. He waited at South Chicago until the **Calumet** arrived. The rescue party was joined by T. P. Calvert from the Chicago Fire Alarm office; Capt. Edward Dionne of the South Chicago Life-Saving Service, and Lieut. Chris Myers of the fireboat **Chicago** stationed in the Calumet River. . . .
>
> After the **Protection** was fairly under way Capt. Consaul said when off Hyde Park crib he saw about three miles east a dark pile, which looked like a hull, with moving figures on it, which he thought might be the **Chicora**.
>
> "We ran out to it," he said, "and found an iceberg fifteen feet high and about as long as our tug, covered with sea gulls and ducks.

TUGS PROTECTION AND CALUMET BUCKING THROUGH THE ICE FIELDS.

All the way down from the river to South Chicago we broke ice from one to three inches thick."

Leaving the Calumet River the **Protection** slipped easily through a few hundred feet of open water and then took its course southeast through a level and solid field of ice. At first the ice was one and one-half or two inches thick and offered little obstruction to the headway of the tug, but as the vessel steamed farther from shore the ice increased in thickness and gradually the progress became slower and slower. . . .

Capt. Dionne of the Life-Saving Service and Lieut. Myers of the South Chicago fireboat kept a lookout with marine glasses on the forward deck for any signs of the wreck. They scanned the horizon in every direction in vain. Except the shore line nothing appeared above the monotonous level of the ice. . . Still the Captain kept on his course unwilling to give up without getting a sight of the object which so many people had seen from the shore. He was inclined to the belief they must have been deceived by some dark spot, perhaps a bit of open water or an iceberg.

Meanwhile the ice became thicker and thicker and the headway slower and slower. When the boat had been out three-quarters of a hour it almost came to a standstill. The engine was stopped and everybody aboard took a look over the ice field through the glasses. No trace of a wreck or a vessel or iceberg or anything that rose above the water level could be seen. Capt. Consaul decided it was useless to go any further and put the boat about and steered for South Chicago. When he had run on the return course a mile or so one of the party looking through a glass said he saw some object between the boat and the shore. The engine was immediately stopped and again everybody took a look though the glasses. Nothing could be seen, however, but the shore line. . . .

It was now growing dark. The shore line had disappeared and a snow storm coming up closed the view on all sides. The Captain lost confidence in his compass and after steaming along for half an hour or more admitted that he did not know where he was. The boat was stopped and the whistle was sounded to signal for the **Calumet**. Every ear was strained to catch the answering signal. But no answer came. Capt. Consaul, Capt. Dionne and Lieut. Myers held a consultation as to what was the vessel's true course. It was decided to hold it northwest, and after sailing in that direction for twenty minutes another stop was made, and the whistle blown again with the same result as before. . . . The wind had either shifted to the east or the compass was wrong and there were several on board who held the opinion that the boat was headed out into the lake.

The third halt and whistle brought a faint answering signal from the **Calumet** and, guided by her whistle the **Protection** made port in South Chicago at 7 p.m.

The news from the tug was the final blow in a series of negative events that had begun shortly after the 7 p.m. extra was published. The 9 p.m. extra edition of the *Benton Harbor Palladium* reflected the growing gloom and included telegrams from two Chicago tugmen which had been received in quick succession about 8:30 p.m. The news caused the request for special trains to be canceled and was headlined:

VERY DOUBTFUL

The body of the report included two new telegrams:

ONE OF MY TUGS AT SO. CHICAGO WENT AFTER THE **CHICORA** AND TWO TUGS FROM HERE NOT MINE. HAVE NOT HEARD OF THEIR RETURN YET, BUT THEY NOR ANY OTHER TUG WILL NEVER FIND HER.
J. S. DUNHAM, PRESIDENT TOWING CO.

THE **PROTECTION** HAS JUST RETURNED AND ITS CAPTAIN REPORTS SEEING NOTHING OF THE WRECK.
H. F. HEATH

The *Daily Calumet* of South Chicago summed up the day, "The mystery of the floating object is yet unsolved, and probably will not be until the lake gives up its dead."

DAILY PALLADI

BENTON HARBOR, MICHIGAN, SUNDAY, FEBRUARY 3, 1895.

SPECIAL, 5 P. M.
BENTON HARBOR, FEB. 2, 1895.

IS IT THE CHICORA?

Hull of Vessel Seen off Chicago.

Said that Signals Indicate Men are alive on board.

Tugs and Relief Party Sent out from Chicago.

Reported that Her Name Can be Read with aid of Glasses.

More News Awaited Here with Breathless Interest.

A condition of profound interest and excitement prevails in Benton Harbor this evening over the receipt of telegrams regarding the lost steamer Chicora.

The first dispatch that startled the

SPECIAL, 7 P. M.
BENTON HARBOR, FEB. 3, 1895.

IT IS THE CHICORA!

Hull of Vessel Seen off Chicago.

Said that Signals Indicate Men are alive on board.

Tugs and Relief Party Sent out from Chicago.

Reported that Her Name Can be Read with aid of Glasses.

More News Awaited Here with Breathless Interest.

A condition of profound interest and excitement prevails in Benton Harbor this evening over the receipt of telegrams regarding the lost steamer Chicora.

The first dispatch that startled the

EXTRA!

Benton Harbor Feb 3.

Nine O'clock P. M

VERY DOUBTFUL

Later Reports Less Encouraging About Finding Chicora.

Tugs Returning Without Seeing the Wreck

Possibility that the Earlier Reports Were Cruelly Untrue.

More News Awaited Here with Breathless Interest.

A condition of profound interest and excitement prevails in Benton Harbor this evening over the receipt of telegrams regarding the lost steamer Chicora.

The first dispatch that startled the city from its Sabbath quietness was the following, received by Mr. E. E.

*The **Chicora** headlines from the three special editions of the Benton Harbor Daily Palladium. The newspapers were issued at 5 p.m., 7 p.m. and 9 p.m. on Sunday, February 3. The stories were published on an inside page, the normal location for local news.*

17

The Spark Extinguished

Monday, February 4

Clerk W. J. Hancock who was still at Saugatuck received a wire from Graham and caught the night train that passed through Benton Harbor about 3 a.m. Monday. He conferred briefly with Graham and was sent on to South Chicago where, peering through the darkness, he could barely make out the ice floes on the lake. The next morning Hancock sent two telegrams, the first at 9 a.m., the second two hours later, and, according to the *Benton Harbor Palladium* editor, "blew away every spark of remaining hope in the minds of the aroused community:"

> Chicago, Feb. 4, 9 a.m.,
> HAVE TALKED WITH CAPTAIN OF THE TUG **PROTECTION**. HE SAYS HE SIGHTED THE OBJECT OFF WHITING THAT WAS SEEN FROM SHORE; WENT TO IT AND FOUND IT TO BE WINDROWS OF DARK ICE. WILL WIRE IN A SHORT TIME.

> Chicago, Feb. 4, 11 a.m.
> NO FURTHER NEWS. THERE IS NO FOUNDATION FOR THE STORY MORE THAN I WIRED. WE WILL START IMMEDIATELY WITH THE TUG **MORFORD** AND COVER THE COURSE AS YOU ORDERED.

During the brief train stop in St. Joseph Graham had drawn Hancock a course for the tug to search. Hancock was at the offices of the Dunham Towing and Wrecking Company early in the morning and after an interview with J. S. Dunham, about 10 a.m., Captain George Jewel was ordered to muster a crew and start out on the **T. T. Morford**.

As the February 5, *Chicago InterOcean* describes the trip:

> At 11 o'clock sharp the flagship of the fleet pulled out of the harbor with the following crew: Captain George Jewel; engineer, John Williams; fireman, Edward Burns and lineman, Frank Doyle. The big tug made for the open lake, but found little of it that was not covered with a layer of ice. This averaged, Captain Jewel thought, about five inches all the way, demonstrating that the fall in the temperature had had its effect on the ice since the **Calumet** and **Protection**, twenty-four hours before, had made the trip. The **Morford** was headed for the end of the lake, putting in from midlake for the edge of the heavy shore ice off Miller's Station, Ind. The day was much clearer than Sunday and pretty well the whole territory at the head of the lake was carefully scanned.

THE TUG MORFORD IN THE STORM.

Also aboard, in addition to the tug's crew and Hancock, were M. B. Rice and Doc Ballenger, identified as a friend of druggist J. F. Pearl. Ballenger earlier had been listed erroneously as lost on the **Chicora**.

The *Daily Calumet* reported:

> Undismayed by the certain report from South Chicago that the dark mass out in the lake supposed to be the hulk of the **Chicora** had disappeared, and was thought to be but a dirty, sooty snowbank occasionally the resting place of fatigued gulls, this trio of determined men sat in the pilot house of the **Morford** and told their plans for the search and then took the post of lookout as the tug smashed her way through the drift ice. A crowd on the dock watched the tug until she disappeared in the wilderness of floating ice and then it watched her smoke.
>
> At 6 o'clock last night the tug **Morford** returned. The tug made its way through the ice all the way to Whiting, Ind., and neither on the trip to that place nor on the return was anything seen that in any way resembled the hull of the vessel. It would have been impossible for the vessel to have been in open water Sunday night and been hidden from the view of the men on the tug yesterday.

There was reaction to the supposed sighting of the **Chicora** from all over the midwest. According to the February 6, *Michigan City News*, by the time the report reached that city it was greatly enlarged and included the information that the men could be seen on the boat waving their hats. A little later reports came that entire crew

91

of the **Chicora** had walked ashore at South Chicago and gone into the city.

The *Three Oaks Press* described the scene in its town, "A telegram was received at this place Sunday evening. . . . People were greatly excited over the report and a crowd gathered at the depot Monday morning waiting the arrival of the morning papers. Every person who could get hold of a newspaper held their breath with excitement for a moment but a single glance at the heading of the article blew away every spark of remaining hope."

The *Saugatuck Commercial* for February 8 commented, "Not in recent years has so great a sensation been created in this part of the country as was caused last Sunday by the report of the finding of the hull of the steamer **Chicora** off South Chicago with the crew alive. It cannot be said that among the sailors of which the population of this place is mainly made up the report obtained credence."

The Monday *Benton Harbor Palladium* summarized the events of the weekend under the headline:

CRUEL HOAX!

> The most remarkable thing in connection with the alleged discovery is that scores of marine men with glasses and other people equally reliable under ordinary conditions declare positively that they could see men moving on the raft or a vessel's hull. The object was also seen by the people of Hammond, which is several miles south of Whiting. Newspaper bulletins in the city added to the popular excitement, everybody hoping even against their cooler judgment that the report was true, yet at the same time doubting that human beings could live for two weeks in the freezing weather which has prevailed.

The *Bangor Advance* observed, "It might let in some light on the question to learn just what the glass through which the hull of the **Chicora** was seen off South Chicago last Sunday contained before it was placed to the eye."

After all of the excitement had died down the *Detroit Evening News* commented:

> Not being true, it was a calamity of itself that the rumor was ever born. To kindle hopes that only flicker or glow for a moment and then go out is twice to taste the bitterness of grief and bereavement. The afflicted are revived only to be retortured; the public joy aroused only to be struck dumb again. The victims of the second shock are entitled to profound sympathy for the renewed despair that follows their resuscitated hope. . . . It was a misfortune that anyone was misled into imagining that in some ice flow or berg they saw the effigy of the lost boat, or were perhaps deluded by a mirage. . . The rumors of the resurrected **Chicora**, contradicting all probability, and inconsistent with the prevailing winds and currents on the lake, and all the unknown facts and previous experience of such disasters, make that vessel's fate an incident more memorable than ever in the annals of lake navigation.

18

The Search

One way to get a popular hearing in the area press was to hold out some hope that survivors may yet be found. Captain Ed Napier of South Haven, and Captain Nelson Napier of St. Joseph did so for some time. In the February 6 issue of the *Niles Weekly Mirror*, Captain Paul Armstrong, formerly master of **Sailor Boy** and **Post Boy**, excursion boats around Chicago during the 1893 World's Fair, wrote:

> When the **Chicora** left Milwaukee in fairly good weather, it took the St. Joseph course, southeast. The wind blew up a gale from the southwest. Being at a right angle with the course the boat was put in the trough of the sea. You must now bear in mind that Capt. Stines was an old, experienced and good sea captain. At once he saw that it was impossible to reach St. Joseph and he tried to get back to Milwaukee or to some place of shelter. If he had not lost control of his boat he would have reached the west shore and smoother water, or the only other smooth water he could get to, the lee of its Manitou islands. To go toward Milwaukee would be to lessen the sea by going to the lee shore on the west. To turn toward the Manitous was to have the sea behind him, and in that way he could live in any gale.
>
> The upper works have been washed ashore. If it foundered and sunk these would have gone down with the boat, because in a seaway everything is lashed and made fast. The instances where a boat loses its upperworks and goes to the bottom are hard to find. The upper works did not go off at the first roll, and it looks as if it had shifted them and rolled till it parted the wheel chains. Then everybody went below and waited. Being in the trough of the sea it did not take long to roll these off, and it is likely the smokestacks and breeching to the boilers went with them, and the rudder stock above decks as well. The steering apparatus being gone, the first thing a steamboat man does is to drop anchor, and he does not have to know as much as Capt. Stines to do that, either. The only thing to do was to get holding ground outside the ice or be ground to pieces in the floe. The chances are even that he ran out one anchor chain and shacked the other one to it. This would give them holding ground anywhere in Lake Michigan and far enough from the shore to be safe from the ice. The crew would then be perfectly safe, and there is no reason why they would not be comfortable enough, too. There was plenty of coal aboard and flour enough in the forward hold to feed them for a year and fresh water all around them. They are living there and wondering why some one does not come.

But this view was denounced in most marine circles. The *Evening Wisconsin* responded to the above story, "Those who have hopes that the lost steamer's hull will be found in the ice pack are theorizing without evidence to support any such view. Everything is against them, and they should turn their attention towards the bereaved families of the lost men and endeavor to mitigate their woe instead of deepening it by picturing the possibility of the **Chicora's** existence with a freezing and starving crew in her hold."

The ship's owners were practical men, as soon as it was obvious to them that no man aboard could be found alive President Graham began making announcements that he intended to risk no further lives on the search, but would wait until spring. As early as January 26, the *Detroit Free Press* reported:

> In May, or as soon as the weather becomes more settled a systematic search for the lost steamer and cargo will be established, dragging back and forth in and out for a distance of five to forty miles, spending from four to six weeks if necessary in the search and with the aid of divers attach lines to her and tow her to the shoals where work can be done to remove the immense amount of flour, a great portion of which will come out even then in good condition. The engines and other machinery that can be taken off, including freight that is likely to be found, will be of $50,000 to $75,000 value to them. At present all that can or will be done is to wait for fairer weather before any more work can be done in behalf of wreckage or bodies.

It was expected that the hull would be located in the spring. Graham visited Detroit near the end of February and was quoted in the *Detroit Free Press* as saying that there were several different proposals to locate and raise the vessel. The report went on, "He said if he could find and raise her she could be fitted out for service again this year."

Captain E. E. Napier of South Haven, one of the earliest to find wreckage of the vessel was one of the hopefuls who applied to Graham & Morton for the chance to carry out the search. Napier had once been shipwrecked with Captain Stines, and had a personal reason, although there seemed to be the hope of monetary gain as well. The *Saugatuck Commercial* for February 22, ran a report from South Haven:

> Capt. E. E. Napier of this port has been busy with his plans and figures ever since the **Chicora** was wrecked and he has made up his mind that she is lying within two miles of this port, in water not too deep to make it a paying investment to raise her. He went to St. Joseph and made the company a proposition for the hull, which was not accepted. He then tried to buy a half interest [for $15,000 according to other sources]. One of the officers at St. Joseph went to Chicago to consult with the Chicago owners who decided to have all or none of the **Chicora**, but they were anxious to secure Capt. Napier's services in finding the boat and he secured the contract for finding the **Chicora** for $5,000.

Off. No. 126.902

(Cat. No. 538½.)

CERTIFICATE OF ENROLLMENT
No. 14

OF THE

Propeller

CALLED THE

Chicora

of 1122 ⁹²⁄₁₀₀ net 708 ¹⁵⁄₁₀₀ Tons,

ISSUED AT THE

Port of *Grand Haven*

District of _____

August 19th, 1892

G. W. McBride

Collector of Customs.

DATE OF SURRENDER:

April 29th 1895

WHERE SURRENDERED:

Grand Haven,

CAUSE OF SURRENDER:

Wrecked total loss and papers lost

Jacob O. Eames

D/y Collector of Customs.

2—496

The papers of the **Chicora** *were surrendered just as the search was getting underway.*

There is no further mention of Captain Napier's name in connection with the search but various other boats were made ready. From subsequent accounts it would appear that Graham had decided to search first using his own company's resources. When the **Petoskey** was finally freed from the ice in St. Joseph harbor and left for her first trip to Milwaukee since January special lookouts were posted to locate signs of the wreckage of the **Chicora**.

The *Michigan City News* reported in its April 10 issue: "The steamer **Lawrence** was ready to begin the search for the bodies and wreckage of the **Chicora** Sunday but on account of the dense fog work was postponed not starting until early yesterday morning. . . The beach along this shore is daily being watched by a few idle people who have hopes that some of the bodies might possibly be washed ashore."

The last week of April Captain Rosel Downer, a diver from Chicago arrived in Benton Harbor with his searching apparatus, a two-inch rope, a mile and 700 feet long, with two sinkers, each weighing 150 pounds, placed 200 feet from the ends. With this long cable hanging between them and dragging on the bottom, the tugs **Frank Edward** and **L. S. Payne** would search for the **Chicora**. A reporter from the *Three Oaks Press* quoted Captain Downer as saying that he would "find the **Chicora** no matter where she is in Lake Michigan."

The captain rapidly discovered the task was not so simple, a May 5 report noted, "The searching party looking for the **Chicora** are having much trouble. They find the bottom of the lake covered with snags -- the cable has been broken several times." Newspaper correspondents kept home readers up to date on the search. The first week in May interest was so high that G & M's summer steamer, the **City of Chicago**, took a Sunday excursion from Benton Harbor to watch the search.

At the same time Fred Menier of the fishing tug **Pilot** and George Harvey, owner of the **Elsie**, both based on the Kalamazoo River, were hired by Graham & Morton to cover the area from South Haven to Saugatuck in the same manner. The May 10, 1895, *Saugatuck Commercial* reported: "They are now prosecuting the search with their little fishing tugs, employing a drag so constructed as to float equi-distant from the bottom and surface of the lake. If the **Chicora** is anywhere near this port they will find her." Later the tug **Pup** was also used.

The search was under the direction of W. J. Hancock. He visited his home in Saugatuck in mid-May and the *Saugatuck Commercial* reported that he had four tugs out and "will completely cover the ground from Holland to St. Joseph out to about twenty fathoms. So far nothing has been discovered to give the least encouragement that the boat will ever be found." The work was finally abandoned June 19 "entirely barren of results," according to the Saugatuck newspaper.

But at least one man was not convinced. The *InterOcean* for October 22, 1895, published the following:

> "There is no doubt in my mind that the Graham & Morton Transportation company knows exactly where the wrecked steamer **Chicora** lies, and moreover, it does not intend to raise her before the expiration of a year from the date she was lost."

The foregoing statement was made yesterday in the Templecourt building by F. A. Makin of Allegan, Mich., who, according to his business card is "Promoter and General Manager of the Fruit Belt Line, Holland, Saugatuck & Southeastern Railroad company."

"What is the object of the company in not raising the steamer?"

"Under the law as I understand" replied Mr. Makin, "if the steamer is not found within a year from the time she was wrecked, according to the terms of settlements made with them, the consignors will have no claim on the cargo. The **Chicora** went down with from $15,000 to $20,000 worth of flour. As everybody knows it would not be wet more than half an inch from the outside; all the rest of the flour would be as good as new. That flour if raised would be worth from $7,000 to $12,000."

"I was on one of the tugs when the Graham & Morton company was dragging the lake for the **Chicora**. The chain caught on some obstruction too heavy to lift and broke. A diver was sent down to see what it was. As soon as he came up before his armor was removed he was taken directly to the cabin where the official of the Graham & Morton company was. When the diver came on deck he was asked what he had found, he laughed and said: 'Oh, it was only a stump,' or something of that kind. I was satisfied then and am now that he found the **Chicora** and received instructions when in the cabin to keep his mouth shut."

"Where do you think the vessel lies?"

"She lies at a point about eleven miles northwest of St. Joseph and about ten miles west by south of South Haven. If these courses are run out I'll wager the vessel is found within forty rods of the place they cross."

As further proof of his statement Mr. Makin said: "Whenever there has been a heavy northwest wind wreckage from the **Chicora** has been thrown ashore at Benton Harbor, Riverside and Stevensville. With a west wind the wreckage is cast up at South Haven. These facts alone would indicate about the location of the wreck."

Officials of the Graham & Morton company ridicule the statement of Makin and declare that they would raise the **Chicora** at once if they knew where she was.

On April 29, 1895, the enrollment of the **Chicora** was surrendered at Grand Haven, and her fate was entered in the official record as "Wrecked, total loss and papers lost."

19

Eyewitnesses

If the weather had been better, there would have been many people out on the shore scanning and listening for the overdue steamer. But a blizzard was prevailing, whipping blinding snow ashore with winds of up to 50 miles an hour. Even in those circumstances there were several people who either saw or heard, or thought they saw or heard, the **Chicora** attempting to make port in St. Joseph between Monday night, January 21, and Wednesday, January 23.

* * *

There were a number of people along the shore who heard, above the wailing wind, a sound that they believed to be a steamship whistle that might have belonged to the **Chicora**.

The St. Joseph newspaper for February 2 reported, "The steamer's whistle was heard plainly by Engineer McAnte of the tug **Tramp**, stuck in the ice a few miles off shore of St. Joseph with mountains of ice piled about her, about 7 p.m. Monday; about the same time it was heard by Mr. Bundy, at his home in Hagar, and Mr. Vanderveer, in Watervliet, both living near the lake. "All these parties are people who have the confidence of those who know them and it is said their statements in this case can be relied upon as worthy of credence."

The Thursday, January 24, issue of the *Benton Harbor Palladium* noted: "Mr. W. N. Bundy, living north of Pike's Pier, was in this city Wednesday and stated to Dr. Bostick that some time in the early part of the night Monday he heard several blasts of a boat's whistle near his place, and if such is a fact the vessel was undoubtedly the **Chicora**. Mr. Bundy said he remarked to his wife at the time that it was strange a boat should be so close to shore at that distance from a harbor."

The January 30, 1895, *Buchanan Record* commented, "Mr. Bundy's story is generally believed. He said he heard a boat whistling off Pike's Pier early Tuesday morning and it is thought that the **Chicora** was near that point and in distress. So near home, and yet lost."

The January 25 issue of the *Palladium* reported, "Mr. Vandervere, a farmer residing east of this city, reported that on Monday night after going to bed he heard a steamer's whistle in the direction of Riverside which he believes to have been the **Chicora's**. He says three short blasts were blown and after a brief interval three more. He remarked to his wife that he believed there must be a steamer in distress near the shore."

The April 17, 1895, issue of the *Michigan City News*, responding to a report of an eyewitness that had just been announced, wrote: "A number of our citizens agree that the whistle of the **Chicora** was distinctly heard off this port a little before 7 o'clock on Tuesday morning, January 22nd, blowing distress signals, and a number came up town to see if it was not one of the F. & P. M. boats coming into this port with a load of salt as had been their custom winters before. The sound of this heavy boat whistle was distinctly heard here as above stated, by W. T. Kimsey and family, residing over the First National Bank, and by M. A. Howe and family and a number of others, who went out in that terrible storm and gale to see if it was not the salt boat, or some boat driven in here by the terrible storm, then raging upon the lake. But no boat arriving, it was concluded she must be lying outside. Between the hours of 9 and 10 o'clock of that day the same whistle was again heard off to the northwest of this port by many of our citizens, which was the last signal sounded, so far as anyone in this city knows."

* * *

Henry R. Goss, 16 years old in 1895, was on a farm at Paulville, seven miles south of South Haven. His story was generally discounted at the time. "Nobody would believe I heard the horn until the next spring, when some 100 barrels of flour floated up on the beach nearby."

He recorded a full version of his story for Irving K. Pershing, who was later a columnist for the *Commercial Record*, published at Saugatuck. Pershing used the story in a 1993 column without giving the writer's name:

>My home at that time was one mile back from the lake and at that time was called Paulville or Packards Pier now known as Palisades Park, about seven miles south of South Haven and three miles west of Covert. The day before the **Chicora** went down mother and I went to another farm we owned south of Bangor after a load of corn, 11 miles from one to the other. In the morning of the day the ship went down, I loaded 50 bushels of corn and in the afternoon we started for home. That terrible storm came up and I did not believe we could make it after dark. We should have stayed with someone along the road and I do not remember why we didn't but we finally got home about 9 p.m.
>
>I put the team up and mother fixed us some supper and then I went back to the barn to tend to the horses. While I was in the barn I heard a fog horn blow and on my way to the house I heard it again. That horn was surely blown north of Paulville pier. I told mother there was a steamer on the lake and it sounded as if it was in trouble. That boat was working south. When it went by the opening through the bluffs at the pier it sounded just outside of the icebergs. We had three rows of bergs at that time. We could hear that whistle plainly inside the house with all doors shut. We probably heard it at intervals of 10 minutes for an hour. The last we heard seemed to be different, could have been boilers exploding and I took it to be about one and a half miles south of Paulville. . .
>
>Later I found, hundreds of barrels of flour on the beach, not far from our home and hundreds of cloth sacks of flour. There was a strip of flour about four rods wide and some 50 rods long.

In another telling Goss describes the final horn, "The last blast sounded like one big gurgle, and after that only the sound of the storm was heard."

Some lakeshore residents and fishermen say you can still hear the steam whistle of the **Chicora** on stormy, snowy nights.

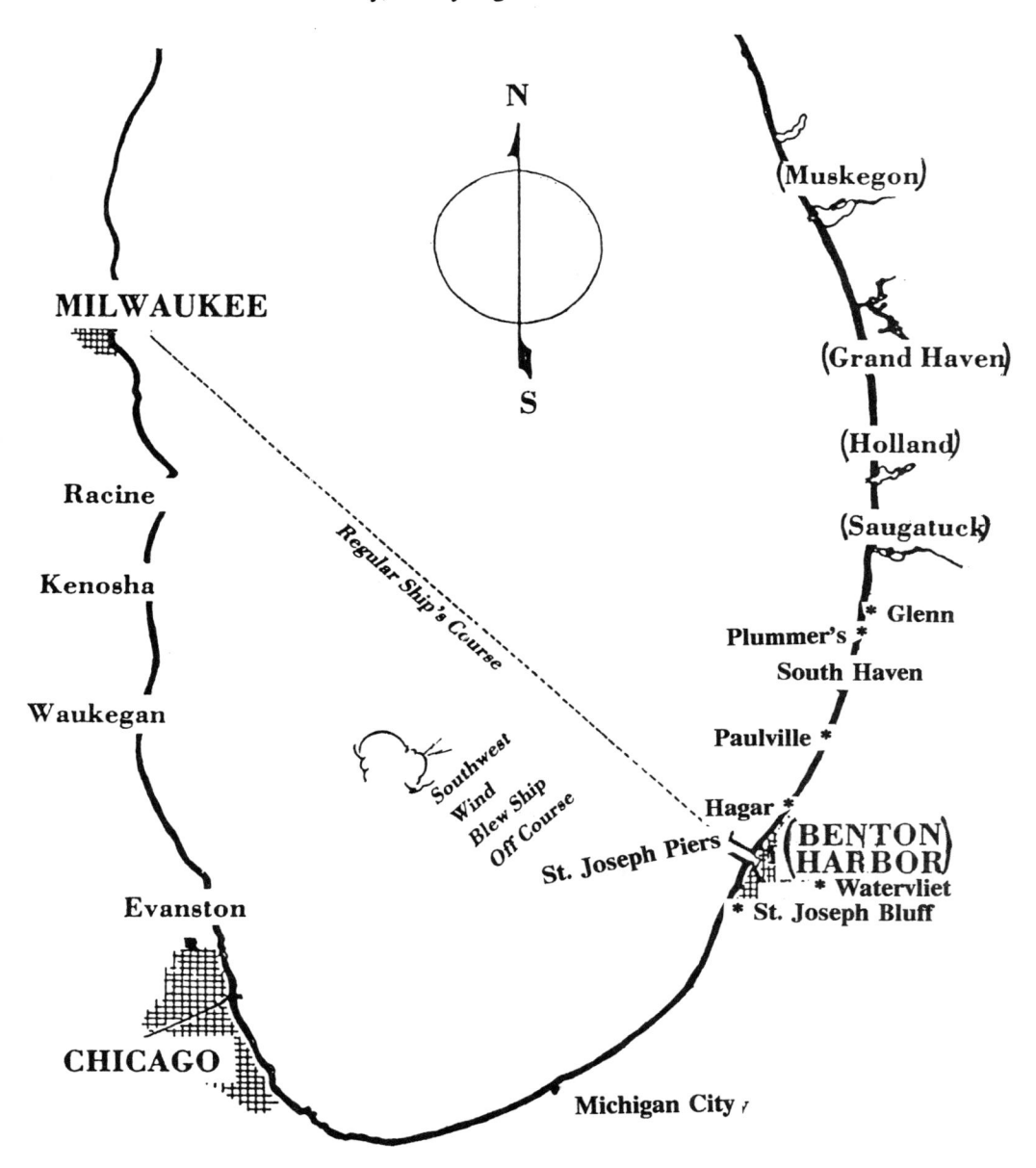

A map of lower Lake Michigan pinpointing reported sightings of the Chicora the cities in Wisconsin are included for reference only.

* * *

There were a few who reported that they actually saw a vessel in the storm:

The January 25, 1895, issue of the *South Haven Messenger* wrote: "Mrs. H. M. Avery reports having seen Monday, a large vessel with a great smoke issuing from her stack which was probably the **Chicora** trying to make headway against the southwest wind." In some later accounts Mrs. Avery is called Mr. Avery.

The *Benton Harbor Daily Palladium* reporter who went to South Haven as soon as wreckage was found wrote, "A lady at the hotel says she saw smoke from a steamer at 2 o'clock off this harbor Monday afternoon. That is about the time she would have been due along here and it is believed by many that it was the **Chicora**." This may be the same Mrs. Avery described above.

* * *

On January 23, 1895, Captain Ed Napier of South Haven sent a telegram to Graham & Morton headquarters in Benton Harbor that Timothy Plummer, a man from the country, had just reported that he "saw a boat at 10 o'clock this forenoon some distance in lake off a point about five miles north of here. He only saw her for a minute."

On Friday, January 25, Plummer was visited by the *Palladium* reporter who wrote, "I went to Tim Plummer's house. He is positive he saw a steamer Wednesday morning off his place and described it as just a hull with no smoke stack. He could not see anything above deck. It looked as though it might have all or part of the promenade deck and was high out of the water, with no spars or pilot house. He saw it three minutes."

Napier said later, "I believe that Plummer saw her. He said he saw a boat without any upper structure. They had probably gone over long before. Headed well up to the norwest, she would naturally chaw round some to the norard, and now I think she will be found not far from South Haven."

* * *

The eyewitness most commonly quoted in respect to the sinking of the **Chicora** was William Hare. The name is also variously spelled Hire, Hair and Higher, it is likely that he was part of the Hiar family, pronounced high-er, of western Allegan County. He was said to live north of Glenn, but a reporter from the South Haven paper drove to the area and later reported that a drive to Glenn "failed to show us any one who knew any such person, or any one who saw the steamer." The *Saugatuck Commercial* identified him as living "on the lakeshore half way between South Haven and Saugatuck" and reported that he went to the offices of the Graham & Morton Company in Benton Harbor and met in early April with Mr. Graham and Chief Engineer William McClure of the **City of Chicago**, a brother of the engineer lost on the **Chicora**. Afterwards a spokesman for the company related his story in a press release:

During the evening of Jan. 23 I was on my way home from Saugatuck. The road runs along the lake shore. When about halfway between the two towns I happened to look out and saw a boat headed for shore. She was not drifting. There was a lull in the storm and my view was unobstructed. It was the **Chicora**, I'm sure. She had high decks and her forward part was well out of water. Her stern was down and looked to be sinking. There were no spars and I saw no signs of life, nor heard signals of distress.

There was no chance of my being able to do anything for the boat and as it apparently was deserted, I went home. A few days after I went back and the boat was then lying on the bottom with her bow up and the ice was pounding her heavily. I paid no more attention to the thing, as I thought that her loss would be known to her owners and everybody else. When I found that the **Chicora** was gone and that no one knew where she had been lost, I was afraid of public censure.

* * *

Allen T. Chesebro, whose family owned Evergreen Bluff near South Haven, was in later years considered the local expert on details of the disaster. He wrote in 1948:

Del Williams, Mr. Avery and Tim Plummer actually saw the **Chicora** at the edge of evening on that fateful night of the 21st between the lull of the blizzard west and southwest of South Haven about five miles out. They could see she was listing badly at a 45 degree angle. It was blowing a gale, sub-zero southwester. The lake was a mass of floating ice then. Del Williams has often told me that when he and Avery first sighted the ship they took position by sighting from the power house smokestack and another object which they never revealed. Del Williams carried this information to his grave.

Far into the night some of the folks could hear the distress whistle. Mrs. A. D. Lewach and Bill Swick said it sounded like a weary fire whistle, but little did they realize that the **Chicora** was desperately calling for help. Being only five or six miles out they must have sighted South Haven lights. There was nothing we could do. Wireless or radio was not known then. Our life saving station was off duty.

Another account by Chesebro describes Del Williams' viewpoint as "from the Old Peoples Home."

* * *

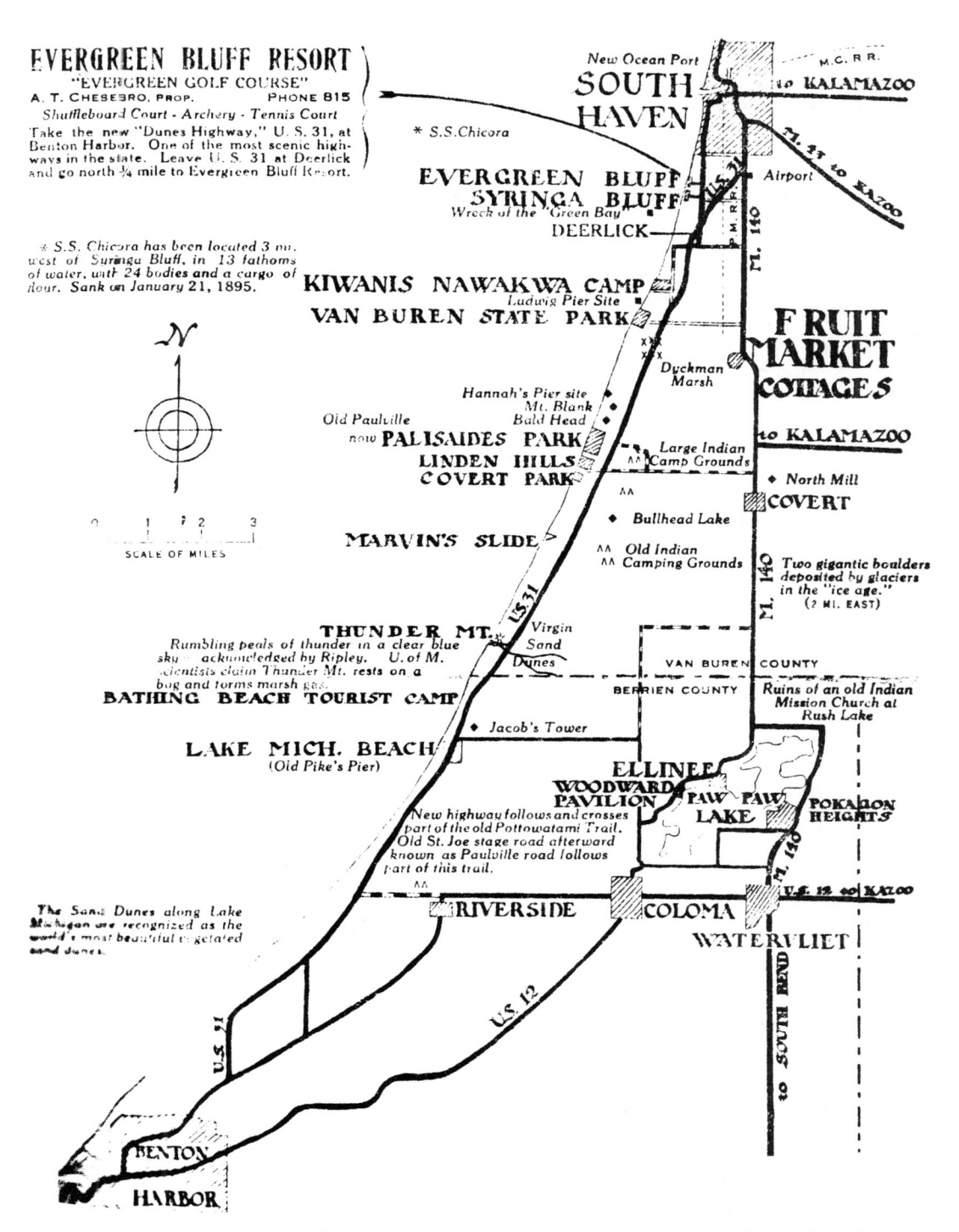

EVERGREEN BLUFF RESORT
"EVERGREEN GOLF COURSE"
A. T. CHESEBRO, PROP.   PHONE 815
Shuffleboard Court - Archery - Tennis Court
Take the new "Dunes Highway," U. S. 31, at Benton Harbor. One of the most scenic highways in the state. Leave U. S. 31 at Deerlick and go north ¼ mile to Evergreen Bluff Resort.

* S.S. Chicora has been located 3 mi. west of Syringa Bluff, in 13 fathoms of water, with 24 bodies and a cargo of flour. Sank on January 21, 1895.

New Ocean Port
SOUTH HAVEN
to KALAMAZOO
M.C.R.R.
* S.S. Chicora
EVERGREEN BLUFF
SYRINGA BLUFF
Wreck of the "Green Bay"
DEERLICK
Airport
KIWANIS NAWAKWA CAMP
Ludwig Pier Site
VAN BUREN STATE PARK
Duckman Marsh
FRUIT MARKET COTTAGES
Hannah's Pier site
Mt. Blank
Old Paulville   Bald Head
now PALISAIDES PARK
LINDEN HILLS
COVERT PARK
Large Indian Camp Grounds
to KALAMAZOO
North Mill
COVERT
Bullhead Lake
MARVIN'S SLIDE
Old Indian Camping Grounds
Two gigantic boulders deposited by glaciers in the "ice age."
(2 MI. EAST)
THUNDER MT.
Rumbling peals of thunder in a clear blue sky - acknowledged by Ripley. U. of M. scientists claim Thunder Mt. rests on a bog and forms marsh gas.
Virgin Sand Dunes
VAN BUREN COUNTY
BERRIEN COUNTY
BATHING BEACH TOURIST CAMP
Ruins of an old Indian Mission Church at Rush Lake
Jacob's Tower
LAKE MICH. BEACH
(Old Pike's Pier)
ELLINEE WOODWARD PAVILION
PAW PAW LAKE
POKAGON HEIGHTS
New highway follows and crosses part of the old Pottowatami Trail. Old St. Joe stage road afterward known as Paulville road follows part of this trail.

The Sand Dunes along Lake Michigan are recognized as the world's most beautiful vegetated sand dunes.

RIVERSIDE   COLOMA
WATERVLIET
U.S. 12 to KAZOO
US 31   US 12
to SOUTH BEND
BENTON HARBOR

Allen Chesebro thought he knew exactly where the boat was when he published this double postcard to advertise Evergreen Bluff Resort in the 1930's.

103

Over the decades additional eyewitnesses continued to surface. In 1957 Arthur O. Scott, 77, who lived in Casco Township, four miles north of Kibbie, revealed that he had seen the **Chicora** in sinking condition the night of January 21, 1895. He said that he waited 62 years to tell his story because, "it never occurred to him that anyone might want to hear me." The following account was published in the March 27, 1957, edition of the *South Haven Daily Tribune*:

> I was 14 years old at the time, and my home then was in Ganges Township only a short distance from the shore. Late in the afternoon I heard a boat whistle and my brother Ward and I went down to the bluff.
>
> It was a dark, windy day, but without rain or snow at the moment. The wind was from the northwest and the beach was completely covered by waves breaking through the ice.
>
> The ship, when we first saw her, was turned bow or stern toward the shore, just north of Crow's Landing. She was about a mile or a mile and a half out.
>
> It looked as though her captain had been trying to head north and had given up and was turning around. In a little while she was heading down wind toward South Haven.
>
> She rocked like a drunken sailor, and her masts and stack dipped toward the water at every roll. We were sure she was done for. The whistle was still blowing, and every now and then she'd throw up a huge black cloud of smoke. We figured water had gotten into her coal.
>
> Sometimes she would be hidden by a wave for a few seconds and we'd hold our breath until she reappeared.
>
> It went on like that for about an hour, and then one big wave blotted her out and we never saw her again.
>
> I can't say for certain that the ship was sunk the moment I lost sight of her. But I know I believed it at the time.

Both of the Scott boys were certain in their identification of the vessel. Arthur said he had been on board the **Chicora** once. He said that the boat had progressed to a point 60 degrees south of a line of sight perpendicular to the shore. That would put her position at the time two or three miles south of Glenn at the time she disappeared, depending on the exact distance between ship and shore.

Crow's Landing is located at the foot of 118th Avenue in Ganges Township, Allegan County, where the Crow family owned 50 acres of land.

After the 1957 newspaper story was published there was an effort to make the 60 degree line proposed by Scott, intersect the powerhouse line that Del Williams had claimed, but there were so many questions concerning both lines that no useful conclusions could be drawn.

* * *

The account brought most recently to public view was written by the granddaughter of Pearl Wyman in a letter responding to an historical story in the *Benton Harbor News-Palladium* in 1988. The writer said:

> My grandmother told me a story about the **Chicora**. She was a young lady then, about 16.
>
> She and her father stood on the bluff in St. Joseph and watched the **Chicora** come within a short distance of the piers, then turn and disappear. The seas were so rough the **Chicora** could not maneuver into the St. Joseph River channel.
>
> Grandmother said they could see the lights on the boat and watched it until it was lost in the high seas and the lights disappeared. It did try to make the channel, but couldn't so it backed off and disappeared.
>
> Yes, the **Chicora** did get to St. Joseph. I never had any reason to doubt her short story. Grandma was there. Her name was Pearl Wyman then, later Mrs. George Pullen of Arden.

* * *

Ghost stories abound in nautical circles and one about the **Chicora** made the newspapers in about 1926. A lakes freighter was traveling north closer to the Michigan shore than the usual shipping lanes. There was a moderate wind and it was snowing when the captain and the wheelsman in the pilot house spotted an old wooden steamer in distress dead ahead. The captain adjusted his course to steer around the vessel and then circled back to investigate but could not relocate the steamer in the storm. When he arrived at the Straits of Mackinac he reported the boat and her approximate location to officials at the Coast Guard station. They asked him for a description. When he finished they eyed him strangely and invited him inside the office. Pointing to an old picture on the wall the officer asked if that was the boat he had seen.

The captain said that was exactly the one and it was a very good likeness. He was told that the picture was of the **Chicora** that had disappeared in the area he described 30 years earlier.

He was so insistent that what he had seen was a real vessel that he came close to losing his license on the basis that he was either drunk or on the brink of insanity.

20

Messages Ashore

A South Haven paper later noted that following the sinking of the **Chicora** "bottles bearing 'last messages' were as common as dead fish on the beach." Nearly all of the finds contained the signature of Robert McClure, chief engineer of the **Chicora**.

According to his friends and family McClure had often spoken of leaving a last message if any disaster should come to his vessel. In late 1894 a special tin box had been made for him by E. Brammall of Benton Harbor to contain such a message. The box was designed to be both waterproof and buoyant. If he carried it on the last trip, and released the box in the water it was never found. All of the messages which came ashore purporting to be written by him were contained in ordinary bottles. To add to the confusion the messages were similar in wording, and it is sometimes hard to distinguish when a newspaper account is talking about a different message, and when it is simply transcribing the words differently.

It was also common for false messages to be thrown into a lake following a disaster, giving the pranksters satisfaction when their fakes were taken as the real thing and written up in the newspapers. Because there were usually more of these fakes than there were real communications, newspapers tended to be skeptical of all bottles that came ashore.

* * *

The first message in the case of the **Chicora** was a bottle picked up near South Haven with a note in it signed "Joe," presumed to be from Joseph F. Pearl, the only passenger. The message said that the **Chicora** was fast sinking and bid goodbye to his wife. But Mrs. Pearl said it wasn't in her husband's handwriting.

* * *

The *Saugatuck Commercial* for April 19, 1895, reported:

> Henry Wells. who lives at Glenn while walking on the lake beach last Sunday saw a bottle floating in the water a few yards from shore. He finally secured it and an investigation found it contained a sheet of paper torn from a writing pad on which the following message was written with a lead pencil: "Our machinery disabled. We could see land if it were not for the snow. Captain and Clarke have been swept over board. We will all be lost; 10:30 o'clock. Good bye. J. D. [sic] McClure." McClure was engineer on the steamer **Chicora** and the supposition on the part of the finder of the bottle was that it came from the ill-fated vessel, and the fact that the cork in the bottle

was packed with cotton waste such as is always in use in engine rooms of steam vessels gave some plausibility to the supposition.

* * *

The *South Haven Messenger of* April 19, 1895, announced the discovery of a bottle along the shore north of South Haven by Henry Wells and Ed Worden. The newspaper went on, "This story at first pronounced a fake by parties in Benton Harbor has since received some credence and is said has convinced them that the wreck lies not far from South Haven; an opinion which has been general among our people for some time."

The April 17 edition of the *Michigan City News*, described the bottle and its contents in detail:

> The bottle was cylindrical in form with a good sized mouth and of a bluish color evidently one of the kind used for bromo-seltzer, and on a piece of ordinary white print paper about three inches long, were written these pencilled words in a small hand:

All is Lost. could see land if not snowed and Blowed. engine give out. drifting to shore. In ice.
                    Chicora   McLure
Captain and Clerk are swept off and we have a hard time of it.
10:15 o'clock.   Good By

On the other side are several rows of partially illegible figures, evidently the score for an unfinished game of pedro and at the bottom the word "chickens."

The note was taken to William J. Hancock who was directing operations from his home in Saugatuck. He wired officials in Benton Harbor and sent the bottle and note there by express. The *Michigan City News* describes the scene when the package arrived:

> When Mr. Graham opened the box, took out the bottle and read the note, the crowd pressed eagerly around his desk to hear every word. Engineer McClure, of the **City of Chicago**, brother of the lost engineer was sent for and when he arrived he took the note to the window and bent over it narrowly scanning the handwriting. As he handed the paper back to Mr. Graham he said decidedly, "Robert never wrote that, sir. That isn't his signature. He wouldn't have written his name like that." He said that his brother would never have spelled his name Mclure: and that he would not have expressed himself as the note read.

However, after searching for handwriting specimens in both the Graham & Morton and American Express offices in Benton Harbor, it was discovered that the engineer sometimes signed his name "McLure," in fact, the *Benton Harbor Palladium* reported, "he signed his name more frequently without the "C" than with it."

The story went on, "Wm. McClure, the lost engineer's brother, who was so positive yesterday that the signature was not that of his brother, was shown a bill on which Robert McClure had written his name McLure and now is inclined to believe that the note is genuine. The authenticity of the message is now accepted by President Graham and others who at first were skeptical chiefly because of Wm. McClure's emphatic denial."

The April 17 *Berrien Springs Journal Era* was sympathetic and wrote of Robert McClure: "He was not known to be a man given to much writing and the circumstances under which he wrote the message -- if he did write it -- were not such as to insure a very good specimen of his penmanship."

The *Buchanan Record* for April 18, 1895, went into some detail about just why the message might be authentic:

> The message, which is now on exhibition at Howard & Pearl's drugstore St. Joe, was written on a piece of white paper about 3 x 6 inches evidently torn from a tablet such as he was accustomed to have tacked up in the engine room and had on the reverse side some pencilling, which looked as though they had kept tally at a game of pedro, which they were accustomed to play while in port. It showed that it was moist when written upon. . . The authenticity of the handwriting had been doubted by William McClure, the engineer's brother, but later development tends to prove that the note is genuine. The leaf on which it was written was torn from a tablet, the same as those supplied the officers of the boats on which to make memoranda reports. On the back of it are numbers pencil marks that were pronounced to be the score of a pedro game. William McClure said his brother was an inveterate pedro player and he wrote the scores of his games just as the tab slip indicates. The fact that the writer signed his name "McLure" caused William McClure to doubt the signature. But yesterday several vouchers signed by the missing engineer for Second Engineer Wirtz of the **Chicora** were compared with the bottle message penmanship and found to be identical.
>
> This message is considered of great importance because it definitely locates the hull of the **Chicora**, to the minds of the veteran sailors in the employ of the Graham & Morton Company. Heretofore Captain Graham has held the theory that the **Chicora** might have sunk at almost any point between New Buffalo on the south and South Haven on the north, a distance of over forty miles. The theory now is that the hull is in comparatively shallow water not very far from South Haven.

It is this note, and the bottle it arrived in, that was photographed and appears on some of the memorial posters, along with a photograph of the boat and pictures of some of the survivors, and other tributes.

In 1953 Harold E. McClure, son of Robert McClure, arrived in Benton Harbor with a note which he said had been kept in the family since the wreck. He stated that it had been purchased from the finder on the beach near South Haven, and not made

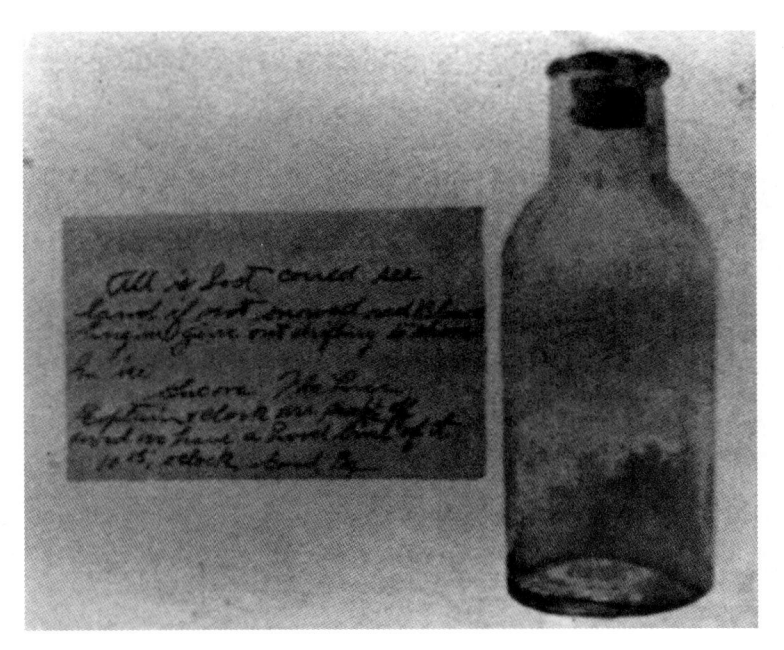

The bottle and note as they appeared on one of the memorial posters issued shortly after the tragedy.

The note produced by Herbert McClure in 1953.

public by the family, but a comparison of the note McClure produced with the note appearing in the memorial posters show that the two are nearly identical except for a frayed edge on the right hand side which might have occurred in 58 years of handling and storage. There are two noticeable differences in the text. An "n" is added to the line "Engines give out" making it more correct grammatically, and an apostrophe making the time "10:15 o'clock."

The son, who was six years old when the **Chicora** went down, said that he was convinced that this particular note at least was authentic.

> First of all, Mother always recognized that note as in Father's handwriting. But there are two other facts that give the note authenticity. First of all, the family name is spelled McClure, but Father always wrote it "McLure" leaving out the second "C." And that's the way it's written on this last message.
>
> Secondly, Father always carried a bottle on his trips which he said he would use to toss overboard a last message if his vessel got in trouble and he thought would founder. He carried such a bottle for years in his work on the Great Lakes and also on Puget Sound.

* * *

The *South Haven Messenger* for April 26, 1895 reported:

> Two men employed by Melville E. Stone at his residence at Glencoe, Ill., picked up on the shore, April 23rd, a preserving jar containing four sheets of paper from a pocket note book rolled up closely and bound with a rubber band. On an inside page was written. "Chicora engines broke. Drifted into trough of sea. We have lost all hope. She has gone to pieces. Goodbye. [signed] McClure, Engineer."

The *South Haven Sentinel* for April 27, 1895, was skeptical. "Another bottle purporting to be from the Chicora was found on the southern beach of the lake, at Glencoe in Illinois. This was found to contain a message signed by engineer McClure, the same in substance as the one found near Saugatuck. To many it looks as though the unfortunate engineer of a wrecked steamer would be too busy with his machinery to think of writing letters."

21

Wreckage

Wreckage from the lost steamer began to come ashore on Thursday following her disappearance and continued for several years. Fishermen have also netted artifacts that have been identified as part of the **Chicora**. The following list of wreckage found, by date and site has been compiled from written accounts.

1895

Thursday, January 24 at South Haven:

A number of reports mention cabin curtains, partitions between state rooms, pieces of mahogany and baggage room doors.

As reported in the January 25, *Grand Haven Evening Tribune*: ". . . yesterday J. S. Morton one of the investigating committee, returned from South Haven, bringing several boards, door casings and pieces of wood from various parts of the cabin and upper deck, and reported quantities of wreckage floating under the ice and within the slush and many large pieces far out rising and sinking with every billow as it rolls inward."

The *Detroit Free Press*, carried a report in the Friday paper written by one of the delegation of searchers who reported what they found. "We started at 7 a.m. at South Haven and found some of the forward upper bulwarks, went further north and came upon lots of wreckage. Have found pieces from the top of the lower deck, most of the baggage-room, an upper shutter and one life-preserver, but it did not have any name on it. It was torn. Found one barrel of flour, one and a half miles north, which came from the cargo. It was broken. Some of the doors and cabin bulkheads are found supposed to be from room 43, which was near the closet. Much wreckage is in sight farther to the north."

"To a *[Kalamazoo Daily] Telegraph* reporter this morning C. M. Balch, who had just arrived from South Haven, said there was no doubt in his mind that the **Chicora** was lost. He was one of a party who walked two miles out on the ice. He said they found a cabin door and the door of the refrigerator, which was recognized by the regular clerk of the steamer." The newspaper also reported, "Two windows of a peculiar pattern which were in the forward bulwarks of the lost vessel," a large piece floating in open water, and frames of her state room doors and windows, mahogany and fixtures from the upperworks.

New wreckage brought ashore Thursday included hatches, window sashes and interior work of the cabin, several barrels of flour and a life preserver bearing the name **Chicora**. Captain Charles Rickley of South Haven discovered the roof of the hurricane deck, fast in the ice, and actually crawled on top of the section of wood, to satisfy himself that it was from the **Chicora**, a boat he claimed to be familiar with.

Ira Smith of the *Palladium* who was part of the party on the ice on Thursday describes the wreckage they found in some detail:

> Port side upper bulwarks; stanchions 3 1/2 x 3 3/4 inches; outside stringer, 1 3/4 thick; inside ceiling beaded; 1 inch scantling outside bulwarks; ship lap, beaded ceiling.
> In another place we found one of the upper shutters of the passenger gang way.
> We found a broken barrel of flour about one mile west of north from pier, broken up but showing plainly it was from the steamer's cargo; head could not be found.
> Two carlings half mile from barrel, without doubt from cupola in after part of cabin; also some oak, antique finish, and part of some one of cabin bulkheads.
> Further to the northward we found the baggage room door which was cut in half and still further north a great deal more shows up. Little further along found a social hall curtain with hook to hold the passenger shutter up, which was cut in half. This is from the solid work and shows the boat must have gone to pieces above the main deck. Four of these were found about northwest from the pier. We also found parts of drawing rooms 27 and 28.

Also found on this day was a portion of the section of hull that had the words "Benton Harbor and St. Joseph" on it, only the "St. J" was found.

Friday, January 25 at South Haven

Several reports mentioned pieces of the forward upper bulwarks, pieces from the top of the lower deck, most of the baggage room, an upper shutter, a barrel of flour, some of the doors and cabin bulkhead. A forward spar and a piece of wood with "Chicora" on it.

Saturday, January 26 at South Haven

On a day of searching that was curtailed by high winds blowing ice away from shore, and blinding snow, the finds included a steam chest from the kitchen and parts of staterooms.

Monday, January 28 at Saugatuck

Herman Hirner of Saugatuck, then 14, was one claimant for the honor of discovering the mast that was later turned into the Douglas flagpole. On the same trip out on the ice January 27 he found a large piece of the upper deck that was 12 to 14 feet long. Hirner said later he decided that it was too big to carry so he ripped a cabin shutter out of it and brought that ashore.

Tuesday, January 29 at Saugatuck

According to the *Niles Weekly Mirror* found, "two miles south of Saugatuck" were "pieces of the cabin floor, curtains, package [packing?] from the steam pipe, a rounded piece of wood that looked like a corner block of the state room in which the screws were twisted as if the piece had been wrenched off. One mile out in the ice could be seen an object seemingly 20 feet long and 10 feet high, probably part of the **Chicora's** cabin. The searching party did not attempt to reach it on account of the blinding storm and extreme cold."

The *Allegan Gazette* reported that the search near Saugatuck was under the direction of "Mr. Hancock, the clerk who so providentially failed to go on the fatal trip. He has recovered the door to the clerk's room which he will retain as a momento, and some of the signs over other doors have been given to relatives of the survivors or to the owners."

By February 9 relics of the salvage work off Saugatuck were beginning to be dispersed. The Allegan newspaper reported, "A piece of wreckage from the steamer **Chicora** is on exhibition in Grice & Gay's window. It was left there by a Mr. Clements from Saugatuck. Sheriff Stratton has a piece from the pilothouse of the same boat and on it is a fine brass lock in perfect working order. He values it very highly."

The purser's box found in the sand near Saugatuck and the door knob and lock removed from the pilothouse door, the wood has cream paint on one side, foam green on the other.

One of the duties assigned to county sheriffs in Michigan is to oversee the recovery of bodies and goods that wash ashore following disasters on the lakes. Sheriff Joseph Stratton of Allegan County took his duties very seriously and he and his deputies spent many hours patrolling the shore. Stratton family records include a scrapbook about the **Chicora** incident that included newspaper clippings and letters from the families of the victims inquiring about specific bodies and giving the official names of those to contact if the remains were found. The pilothouse door section with the brass lock, discovered near what is now the West Side County Park, and the purser's box, found empty in the sand, were later given by his wife, Anna, to the Allegan County Historical Society Museum, where they remain on display.

* * *

There was a break from further discoveries as the ice solidified and snow hid the debris. Later, when the ice began to break up, walking around on it was very dangerous, but with the full spring breakup wreckage began to float about in the lake and wash ashore.

March 22

Reported in the *Saugatuck Commercial*: "The ice on Lake Michigan near the St. Joseph shore line is beginning to waste away and wreckage which has been covered by it is now being recovered. Within a day or two parts from around the engine room and the chair which Chief Engineer McClure used have been found.

April 5

Near Holland, north of Saugatuck, some canned goods were found, as well as flour and pieces of upper works.

North of St. Joseph a piece floated ashore which was identified as a forward gangway.

In the "spring" at Paulville: hundreds of barrels of flour, hundreds of cloth sacks of flour, strip of flour four rods wide and 50 rods long.

April 10

Reported in the *Michigan City News*: "The captain of the steamer **F. & P. M. No. 1** reports sighting in an ice field in mid-lake yesterday, timbers, planks and other parts of a steamer supposed to belong to the **Chicora**. No bodies seen. The ice field was large."

April 12

"Wreckage is being picked up all along Lake Michigan."

April 14:

The scene at New Buffalo as reported in the *Three Oaks Press*:

> Since the wind has shifted **Chicora** wreckage is coming ashore in vast quantities here this afternoon. A large piece of the roof of the pilothouse was found. It had been chopped away from the sides of the pilot-house, showing plainly that the crew had made an effort to save the noble craft. The piece is several feet square, was chopped and splintered at both ends and torn from its side fastening. The finding of these pieces of wreckage has caused the citizens of this quiet village to turn out in crowds upon the beach. A conductor of the Chicago and West Michigan Railway train reports that he is positive that he saw the body of a man supposed to be from the steamer floating near shore. He reported it to the authorities this morning as soon as possible, but upon their arrival it had disappeared. As there is a heavy current near the outerbar his story is credited, and it is thought that the body was carried outside of the bar by accident. . . The front flag staff was found Saturday afternoon and the lid of a sailor's chest this morning, also several broken clothes baskets and portions of chairs and stools. Wreckage is found in such large quantities that people with wagons are gathering it up for firewood.

Some reports indicate that the body which was seen at New Buffalo and then disappeared in waves before it could be secured had dark-colored skin and may have been one of the Negro crewmen. It was seen only at a distance and the darkened skin might also have been caused by drowning and decomposition.

April 17

Reported in the *Michigan City News*:

> Frank Krueger picked up a life preserver about four miles up the east beach yesterday afternoon. The letters "Chic" were still on the preserver and the letters "ora" were partly washed off but an impression of them still remained. One cork was also missing from it, but aside from this the preserver was practically in a good condition. More wreckage is reported to be on the beach about the same distance out. The propeller **Roanoke**, which arrived in port yesterday afternoon from Manistee sighted considerable **Chicora** wreckage on her trip. Cabin work and deckage were seen about thirty miles off this port, and broken wreckage of all description was floating in mid lake.

PICKED UP A CHAMPAGNE BOTTLE.

The tug **Diamond** picked up a large bottle about half filled with the beverage about ten miles out in the lake yesterday. The bottle was still securely corked and was probably off the **Chicora**.

April 18

Reported in the *Michigan City Dispatch*:

Carl Brimmer, son of Henry Brimmer, found Sunday a lot of **Chicora** wreckage on the beach west of the city, opposite what is known as the tamarack "swamps." Out of this wreckage he picked up and brought home half of a life-preserver, which is the most important relic thus far found, for it tells a brief story of preparations made aboard the ill-fated steamer by one man at least to escape the fury of the awful storm. The life preserver had been in use, for two of the strings are tied with a knot just as the man had tied it when he fastened the life preserver around his breast and shoulders.

The **Belle Chase** Saturday afternoon found a piece of mahogany casing from one of the doors of the **Chicora**. Three brass hinges were attached to it. The relic was found near the fishing grounds about twenty miles out. Johnson Bros. have these for sale.

April 19

The *Three Oaks Press* also reported the portion of pilot house but added the detail that the fragment had the letters "Chi" clearly visible, and that the relic was on display at G. M. Wart's grocery store in New Buffalo. "G. A. Humiston a traveling man, came to this place from New Buffalo and he brought with him three pieces of mahogany panels which he picked up on the beach. They attracted a great deal of attention and every one seemed anxious to get a look at them."

April 24

The *Michigan City News* reported:

A Floater at New Buffalo

The body of an unknown man which had been washed ashore from the lake was picked up on the shore near New Buffalo yesterday afternoon about 4 o'clock. No one has yet been able to identify the remains, although they are believed to be those of one of the victims of the late **Chicora** disaster. There was nothing on the body by which to identify it. . . A pocket knife, keys and a handkerchief were taken from the pockets of the clothing and sent to Benton Harbor for identification. The remains are believed to be those of Stein [sic] or Pearl, lost with the **Chicora**. They were badly decomposed and were temporarily interred at New Buffalo today.

The *Three Oaks Press* reported "Tuesday morning the body of a man was picked up on the shore about 3 miles from New Buffalo. The body was minus coat and vest. On his person was found $2.45 and a bunch of keys. The only possible clew by which he could be identified were the initials C. P. E. marked on the linen he wore. The body measured five feet, seven inches, in height, estimated weight, 140 pounds. Persons from St. Joseph and Benton Harbor went to new Buffalo and viewed the remains but failed to identify the same as belonging to the **Chicora**."

The body was never identified with any certainty. The May 3, 1895, *Saugatuck Commercial* said: "The identity of the body of a **Chicora** victim found at New Buffalo is not yet established, a report from Niles that it was that of C. H. Stone to the contrary notwithstanding. Wm. McClure is still inclined to believe that the remains are those of his brother Robert, while others are equally confident that the body is that of First Mate C. D. Simons. Near the end of May the remains were disinterred again at the request of James McClure, but "after a careful investigation Mr. McClure was unable to identify the remains."

* * *

Even after things had settled down following the spring break-up, wreckage continued to float around in the lake, and new pieces were discovered after every storm.

May 17

In a story with a Benton Harbor dateline: "Several pieces of **Chicora** wreckage picked up late today at Devil's Hole, one mile north of here on the lake shore with silver trimmings attached, showing that it came from the clerk's office and main deck. The moldings bearing the silver bracket showed a recent break as though torn off by late washings of the waves."

The South Haven newspaper reported: "Last Sunday a sack of flour was found in the water some distance down the beach, and on Wednesday, Capt. Donahue found another partly empty, a little south of the pier, both undoubtedly from the wreck of the **Chicora**." A shade roller was also among the finds. Later in the week a baker sent the editor a slice from a loaf of bread that had been made from flour picked up on the shore. "It was as nice as if it came directly from the mill."

May, 24

In late May more flour was discovered on the South Haven shoreline, and, at St. Joseph, a part of a cabin and some furniture.

June 7

The South Haven newspaper reported: "Another sack of flour was found on the beach south of the pier last week by Jimmie Donahue, supposed to have come from the ill-fated **Chicora**."

July 2

In Ganges Township south of Saugatuck a South Haven newspaper reported, "Since the storm of Friday three sacks of flour, a ship buckle and several incandescent lamps were washed ashore at Pier Cove. The point on the shore where the articles were found is opposite the place where the searching parties' drag caught when they were searching for the sunken hull."

November 1

At St. Joseph: "A large quantity of wreckage, mattresses, chairs, etc., has blown into St. Joseph since the last storm."

November 2

The *Benton Harbor Palladium* reported: "A man rode along the north beach about 11 miles Friday on his wheel and found a flour barrel partially filled with flour, some canned goods and pieces of wreckage. Among the pieces were some strips of molding similar to those in the cabin of the steamer **Chicora** and which were painted the same color. He also found a round piece which looked as though it had been around a spar on the upper deck."

* * *

For many years any high winds or turbulent storm seemed to shake loose more wreckage. Other pieces of the boat and her fittings have been brought up in the nets of fishermen. As wave action has broken what is left of the vessel and her cargo into smaller pieces they are more difficult to identify, but it is possible that some items seen on the shore today come from the wreck of the **Chicora**.

January 17, 1901

An unidentified marine record column in an old scrap book notes, "The wreck of the **Chicora** lies 10 miles to the southwest of St. Joseph. This was confirmed by finding a bunch of brass baggage checks."

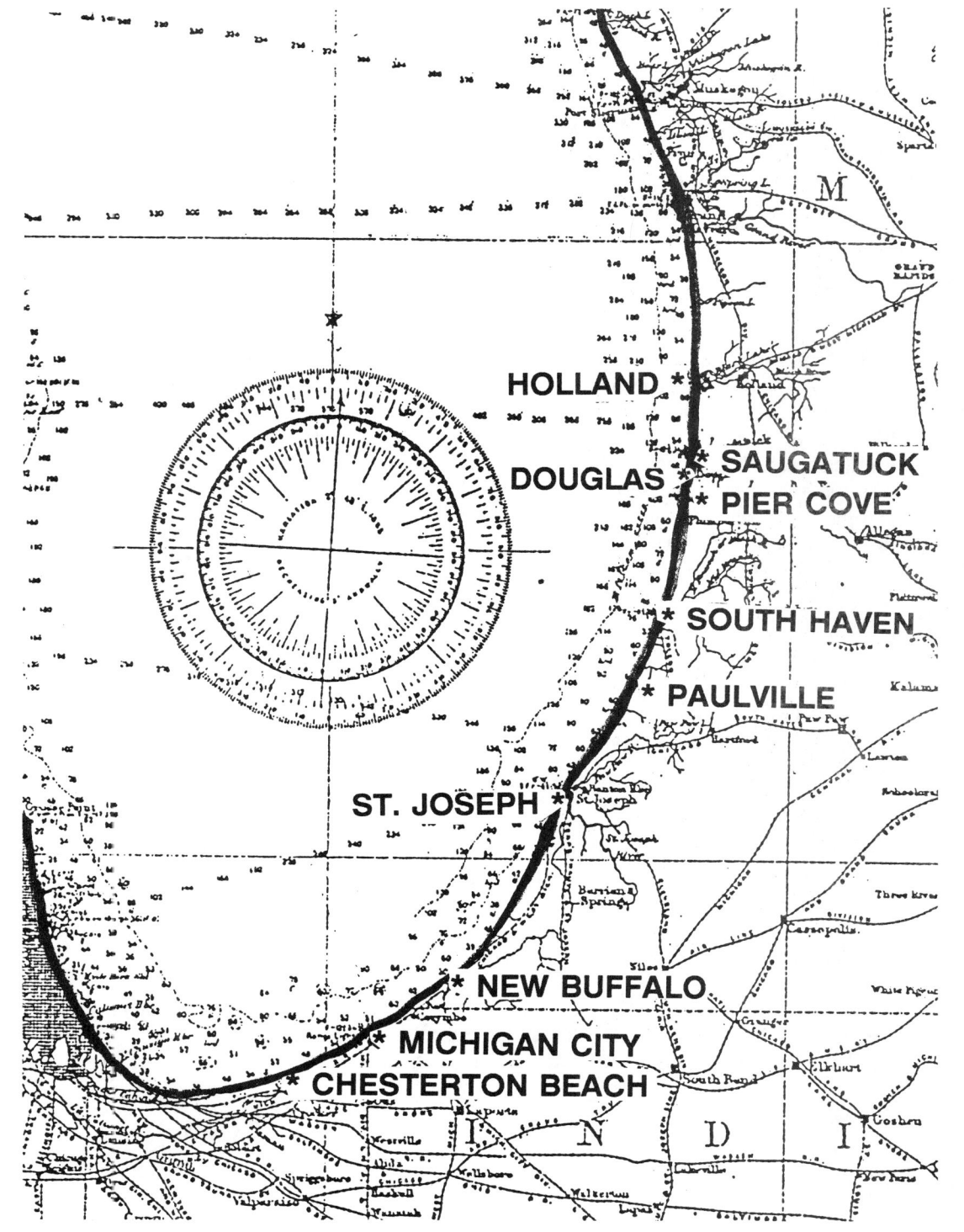

A map of the east coast of Lake Michigan marking sites where wreckage from the Chicora has come ashore or been found.

September 8, 1905

A report in the *Michigan City News* said, "John Lessor, a farmer near Bluffington, Indiana, found near his place a piece of wreckage from the steamer **Chicora**. It was of wood about 15 feet long and had the initials G & M and the name Chicora."

April 20, 1917

A story in the *South Haven Tribune-Messenger* reported wreckage that had been pulled up in fish nets and brought to port by the tug **Herbert**, owned by Mollhagen & Co. "A washbasin and electric light fixture, both stamped 'Chicora' that were pulled up by fish nets, were identified by Captain J. A. Simons and Captain Russell, of the Graham & Morton fleet as belonging to the **Chicora**. Later an inch cable was pulled to the surface. The electric light fixture was manufactured by the Bryant Manufacturing Company, a firm which has been out of business for 15 years. The wreckage lies in about 35 fathoms of water, about 10 miles from St. Joseph. -- a buoy has been placed to mark the spot." According to Great Lakes historian, George Vargo, for years Captain Charles Mollhagen of St. Joseph, a fisherman, when asked would declare that the wreck was in 32 fathoms of water, about 10 miles from shore.

1932-1933

Allen Chesebro wrote in 1955, "Back in 1933 Jerry Jedlicka and his son, George, got their nets caught on something three or four miles off shore in 85 feet of water. With their grappling hook they got yellow paint on the points. The second time they pulled up a chair. It was covered with slimy coating. Being under the water for nearly 40 years it was well preserved. But they threw it back. It would have proven a valuable identification of the **Chicora**. Jedlicka, thinking that the flour would be worth salvaging by being sealed by a coat of flour paste put in a claim."

Another account of the same incident noted that Jerry Jedlicka first located the wreck in September of 1932, and that it was found again the following spring by Jedlicka and "other fishermen in the same locality."

One of the most macabre stories, from an undetermined source, is that many years after the wreck a faded blue sailor cap with the initials G and M on it and a skeleton hand still clinging to it was found on the Michigan shore.

20

The Victims

About three weeks after the disappearance the *Benton Harbor Palladium*, the *St. Joseph News* and the *Benton Harbor Banner-Register* all published Memorial Editions with the full story of the tragedy and obituaries and tributes for the crew members and passenger lost with the **Chicora**. Portraits were included for many of the men. These portraits and a picture of the boat, were also combined to print a memorial poster. The biographies below are based on the memorial editions, with additional material from other sources.

Edward Stines, captain

Edward George Stines, 47, of St. Joseph was captain of the **Chicora**. He was born in Saratoga, New York, in 1848, and came to St. Joseph with his parents as a child.

He began work on the Great Lakes at the age of 14, sailing first on schooners, and then worked for Goodrich as mate on one of their large passenger steamers.

In 1868 Stines narrowly escaped death when the **Guide** spent three months icebound in Lake Michigan, seven miles off St. Joseph. Captain Ed Napier was also on the **Guide** and his friendship with Stines may have partially motivated his later efforts to find the hull of the **Chicora**.

At the time of his death Stines had been employed by the Graham & Morton line for 17 years beginning as master of the steamer **Skylark**, and later sailed on the **Messenger, Lora** and **Puritan**. Prior to the construction of the **Chicora** Stines served a short time as captain of the **City of Chicago**. He was the only captain the **Chicora** had known in regular service.

Edward G. Stines, Captain

He was married April 10, 1870, and had one son, Benjamin Edward, who was second mate on the **Chicora** and also perished. At least one brother, Henry, who was a captain for the Goodrich line, and at least one sister, Mrs. Morris, who resided in Chicago, survived him along with his aged mother.

The memorial edition quotes "an old sailor who knew him well" who said, "Captain Stines was a brave man who knew his business as well as any man who sails. . . He was rather reserved in disposition, yet always kind and accommodating and the thousands of people who crossed the lake year after year learned not only to put their fullest confidence in his seamanship, but to regard him as a personal friend whose memory they will cherish long and well."

One of the first newspaper stories out of Benton Harbor on January 23, 1895, the day the first wreckage was discovered at South Haven, reported: "Capt. Stines is said to have had forebodings of impending disaster and some time ago said as much to friends." If this is true he did nothing about it. A later biography printed in the *Palladium* noted, "Captain Stines was a member of a shipmasters' beneficiary order in Chicago in which he carried $1,000 insurance, but unfortunately he had recently allowed his policy to lapse and it is a question whether anything will be realized on it." Another report included the information that he had just completed paying off the indebtedness on his residence three weeks before leaving for the fatal trip. His home was on State Street in St. Joseph.

Cornelius D. Simons, first mate

Cornelius D. Simons (West Michigan newspapers often spelled his name Simonds, but Detroit newspapers usually left off the d), 41, of Benton Harbor, was first mate of the vessel, second in command after the captain. He was born near Oakville, Canada, August 8, 1854, and moved to Alpena, Michigan, at the age of 7, and to Benton Harbor with his family in 1868. He had worked for the Graham & Morton Company for over 20 years beginning as a cabin boy. The employment was continuous except for one season when he served on the **Mabel Bradshaw** and another season on the **Maxwell**, between Pentwater and Ludington.

He was married in 1882 at South Bend to the former Ollie Chadwich, and had a ten year old son, Cornelius A., called "Allen." He was also survived by two brothers, Bert Simons, first mate on the **City of Chicago**, and Del Simons of Grand Rapids.

C. D. Simons, First Mate

"Everyone who knew him liked Neil Simonds, who was a kind husband and father, an exemplary man, and his sunny nature shed constant pleasure wherever he went.'

Benjamin E. Stines, second mate

Benjamin Edward Stines, 24, of St. Joseph, was following in the nautical footsteps of his father. He was born in St. Joseph, July 17, 1871, and began work on the boats at 13 years of age as a cabin boy, working himself up until he received his papers as second mate.

Even at his young age shipwreck was not unknown to Bennie Stines. About 1890 he was a member of the crew of the barge **Ohio**, in command of Captain Robert Evans, when the vessel wrecked on northern Lake Huron. Stines and others took to a life boat and landed on some of the islands, finally reaching Chicago and then St. Joseph after all had been given up for dead.

The memorial edition said, "Bennie . . . was a young man of excellent habits, attentive to duty and fond of his avocation and he will be mourned by many acquaintances besides the doubly bereaved mother who is now left alone in the world."

Benjamin E. Stines, Second Mate   *Joseph Marks, Wheelsman*

Joseph Marks, wheelsman

Joseph Marks, wheelsman, was born in London, Ontario, Canada, but orphaned at an early age and went to live with an uncle until he was 11, then moved

123

to Meaford, Ontario, Canada, where he lived with Angus McIntosh until he became at sailor at 16 and served on various tugs and schooners on the Great Lakes.

In 1888 he discovered that his sister, Mrs. Jay Pike, was living in St. Joseph and in 1893 journeyed to see her for the first time since he was a child. He liked the area and decided to move to Michigan, obtaining employment as wheelsman on the Graham & Morton boats **City of Chicago** and, later, **R. C. Reid**. When the **Chicora** was fitted out for her last trip to Milwaukee, he took the wheel, but had made all arrangements to take a vacation with his sister afterwards to visit relatives in Canada. A sister and a brother in Canada were among his survivors.

The memorial edition summed him up, "He was a young man of exceptionally good habits, of a rather retiring disposition, his circle of acquaintances being consequently limited."

James R. Clarke, clerk

Clerk James R. Clarke, 50, was perhaps the most famous of the crew. He had served as U. S. marshal for the western district of Michigan, headquartered in Grand Rapids, and was a former sheriff of Berrien County.

Clarke was born February 21, 1844, in Montreal, Quebec, Canada, of Scottish descent. The family immigrated to Michigan in the fall of 1843 and settled in Battle Creek.

During the Civil War he served for two years in the U. S. Telegraphy corps. After his return, in 1866, he was married to Alethia H. Goodrich and worked for the Goodrich Transportation Co. from 1868 to 1875.

He was deputy sheriff of Berrien County until 1880, when he was elected sheriff and served four years, at the same time working with the Graham & Morton Co. When his term as sheriff was over he was regularly employed by the company on the **Lora, Puritan** and other boats until appointed U. S. Marshal in 1890, a post he held under February of 1895.

In the St. Joseph area Clarke was known as a sportsman. He played baseball for several years with a local team and was an accomplished skeet shooter.

He was married and had recently built "a fine residence on one of the fashionable streets in St. Joseph."

James R. Clarke, Clerk

The couple had one daughter, Mrs. Della Mitchel of Chicago. Clarke was a 32nd degree Mason, a member of the Mystic Shrine of Grand Rapids, a charter member of Malta Commandery, No. 44, Knights Templar of Benton Harbor; and a member of the St. Joseph Lodge of the Ancient Order of United Workmen in which he carried $2,000 insurance.

Thomas Robertson, watchman

Thomas Robertson, 28, of Baltimore, Maryland, was not well known in Benton Harbor. His father, Isaac H. Robertson of Baltimore, apparently in answer to a request from the Benton Harbor newspaper, sent in a brief sketch of his son's career for the memorial edition.

"Thomas Robertson was born in New York City, April 20, 1866, and moved to Baltimore in September, 1869. After going partly through the public schools he helped his father in the latter's store in Baltimore. When he was 21 he made up his mind to go West and first went to Ottawa, Kansas, where he stayed for two years. In 1889 he went to Chicago and became a sailor. He seldom wrote home, so that his father knew little of his life. Last December he wrote from St. Joseph that he was working for the Graham & Morton company and his father, reading the son's name in the papers in connection with the loss of the **Chicora**, immediately wrote to the company here for further information. The young man was esteemed as a faithful employe and a good comrade."

Merrit W. Morgan, steward

Merrit W. Morgan, 37, of Benton Harbor served as steward. The boat usually carried two stewards, but because there was only one passenger, and a small crew, it was decided that one would be enough. Morgan was born in Bainbridge Township, Berrien County, May 6, 1858, where he lived on the home farm until 1884, except for two years at school at Hartford, Michigan, and one winter when he cooked in a lumber camp in northern Michigan.

He took a business course at Kalamazoo College, 1884 to 1886, and went to Jacksonville, Florida, for his health where he was employed in a hotel and a market. He returned to Michigan and in April of 1893 became steward on the steamer **Mabel Bradshaw**.

Merrit W. Morgan, Steward

In 1894 he took a position as head waiter on the **Chicora** and was acting steward at the end of the regular season. In addition to his father, John Morgan, who remained on the Bainbridge farm, he was survived by a brother, Charles, a Sodus township farmer; his oldest sister, Mrs. H. M. Yendes, a dressmaker in St. Joseph; and siblings, Chloe, George and Edwin on the home farm.

C. B. Wilcox, who was a schoolmate from his Hartford days, wrote: "We happened to be seat-mates during that time, and I learned to love him for his affection and kindness. He was a faithful student and all who knew him were his friends."

Nathan R. Lynch, cook

Nathan Reeves Lynch, 53, of St. Joseph, the cook, was born July 11, 1842, in Steubenville, Ohio. He had worked on boats nearly all his life and for ten years worked as cook on the steamer **Corona**. He came to St. Joseph about 1872 from Milwaukee, and previous to that had sailed in Lake Superior. He had been aboard the steamer **City of Ludington** when she was icebound in Lake Michigan for 16 days in 1883. Lynch began work for the Graham & Morton Company in 1890.

He had an excellent reputation as a cook and was often called on to cater social parties on land.

He and his wife, Sarah, formerly of Cleveland, Ohio, had just celebrated their 26th wedding anniversary. They had no children. The newspaper notes that he carried $2,000 life insurance.

Nathan R. Lynch, Cook   *Jesse C. Davis, Porter*

Jesse C. Davis, porter

Jesse Calvin Davis, 23, was from Benton Harbor and was survived by his wife and one child. He was born near Carthage, Rush County, Indiana, April 1, 1871, and moved to Benton Harbor from South Bend, Indiana, July 22, 1882. He had been employed on the boats in the summers and by J. S. Morton in the winter for several years.

In addition to his wife, the former Florence E. Robinson, and child he left three brothers; Austin B., employed on the **Petoskey**; Elisha, who worked at the Spencer House in Indianapolis, Indiana, and Hawley, of Kokomo Indiana.

The memorial edition noted, "He was a particularly bright and pleasant young colored man who was liked by every one. Mr. Davis was insured against sickness or accident in the U. S. Benefit Society, and the company have already sent Mrs. Davis a check for $100."

Robert McClure, first engineer

Robert McClure, 49, of Detroit, was born November 3, 1845. He served in various positions on steamboats on the Mississippi River and when the Civil War broke out he traveled to Cincinnati, Ohio, to enlist with the First Kentucky Regiment. He fought in western Virginia, at the Battle of Shiloh, South Perryville and Stone River where he was badly wounded and discharged in 1863.

Following the war he served on the **Sandusky**, the **Marine City** and the **Saginaw**. From 1887 to 1890 he worked as a clerk in the U. S. Local Inspector's office in Detroit.

Afterwards he went to Tacoma, Washington, to put a Detroit-built engine in a boat there and was engineer of that boat, running between Portland, Oregon and Tacoma, until January of 1891 when he returned to Detroit.

McClure served first on the steamer **Metropolis**. He had a hand in the construction of the **Chicora** in Detroit in 1892, and sailed with her from the beginning.

He was survived by a wife and five sons, Herbert V. of McClure, Kelsey & Co.; Charles F., in the German American Bank; George R., bookkeeper for McClure, Kelsey & Co.; Robert C., a high school student, and Harold, five years old; and two brothers, George I. and William J. McClure who was engineer of the **City of Chicago**.

First Engineer Robert McClure.

George I. McClure described his brother as, "a man whose life was marked by a strong sense of duty, in the discharge of which he was ever faithful to his trust."

Boat owner John H. Graham told a reporter, "No better or more trustworthy man ever lived than Robert McClure."

Alfred Wirtz, second engineer

Alfred Wirtz, 28, of Detroit, was the only son of Mr. and Mrs. Frank Wirtz of Detroit. He grew up in the city and graduated from a Detroit high school. Wirtz first began working on the Great Lakes about 1888 at the age of 21. By 1892 when the **Chicora** made her maiden voyage to St. Joseph from Detroit he was given the position as second engineer.

After the **Chicora** was laid up in mid December he had gone to Detroit to visit his parents during the holidays but returned to Benton Harbor January 5, in response to the general call for the crew. Wirtz was unmarried.

Second engineer Alfred Wirtz.

William Miller Scheck, fireman

William Miller Scheck, 29, had always been known by his middle name on the employment rolls of Graham & Morton and the addition of another name was a surprise to many. To further complicate matters the name was first printed in the newspapers as Peter Miller. Shortly after the disappearance of the **Chicora** Graham received a letter from George H. Scheck of Upper Sandusky, Ohio, inquiring about his brother William. Graham replied that a sailor named Scheck was not known in Benton Harbor. According to a newspaper report, "A young woman in St. Joseph, a domestic in a boarding house, kept company with Mr. Scheck and has his picture which she showed to Mr. Graham at his home Friday night. He recognized it at once as Miller and telegraphed the matter of identity to the brother of the deceased at Upper Sandusky."

Scheck was born in Philadelphia, Pennsylvania, January 20, 1866. He became a printer in Philadelphia, but quit that trade because of his health and began sailing, first on the ocean and later on the Great Lakes.

He had arrived in Benton Harbor in 1891 and was engaged to be married in June of 1895, to Emma Seasongood of St. Joseph. In addition to his fiancee he was survived by his parents in Philadelphia, and a brother, George, a businessman in Upper Sandusky, Ohio.

The newspaper commented that the fireman "possessed a cheerful, generous nature, was well read, and was esteemed as one of the most faithful of the company's employees." He carried life insurance in the Shipmasters' Union of Chicago.

John A. Werner, fireman

John A. Werner, 29, fireman, was generally known as "the Swede." He had arrived in Benton Harbor from Sweden about 1887, having previously worked as a sailor on the ocean out of a Scandinavian port. Werner had been employed by the Graham and Morton Company for several years.

Shortly after the boat was lost a letter arrived at the post office that appeared to be from his mother in Sweden. It was opened in an attempt to get her address, but there was none, and the postmark read only, "Kil." He was said to have a married sister living in either Chicago or Minneapolis. Werner himself was unmarried.

Grant Downing, oiler

Grant Allen Downing, 26, of Lapeer, Michigan, was born October 26, 1868, at Willoughby, Ohio. He moved to Michigan with his family in 1878 and began his Great Lakes career at Bay City in 1887, surviving a ship wreck his first season. He commanded and was part owner of the steamer **Belle of the Lake** which ran on Long Lake in 1891.

In August of 1892 he shipped from Detroit on the **Chicora**. In January of 1893 he was examined at Port Huron and received a second engineer's certificate, but was employed as an oiler on his last trip.

He was survived by his invalid father, mother, and three brothers.

Grant A. Downing, oiler.

Ralph Downing, coal passer

Ralph Downing, 19, of Lapeer, a younger brother of Grant Downing, oiler, was employed as a coal passer. He was born October 1, 1874, at Willoughby, Ohio, and went on the Lakes with his brother in 1890. He took a season in 1892 to try gold mining in Deadwood, South Dakota, but returned to the Great Lakes.

John G. Hogeboom, watchman

John G. Hogeboom, 37, of Saginaw, who served as watchman, was born in Kalamazoo in August, 1857. His parents died when he was very young and he was adopted by an uncle, Solon S. Goodrich, a banker in Brooklyn, New York. He was educated in Brooklyn and moved to Saginaw where he was employed as a bookkeeper for an insurance company. He worked for a while for the American Express company in Kalamazoo, but returned to Saginaw shortly afterwards and embarked in the drug business with William Keeler, the firm known as Keeler & Hogeboom. He continued in the drug business for about ten years, "having the most popular and best patronized drug store on the West Side," before selling his interest in the store and moving to St. Louis, Missouri. At St. Louis, Hogeboom traveled for a drug firm and later drifted to Chicago where he became a deckhand on the **Chicora** under the name of John Hodges.

He was married in 1883 to Ida L. Crosby of Kalamazoo who, at the time of her husband's death, was living in Saginaw with her young daughter.

James Malone, pantryman

James Malone, about 30, of Chicago, was pantryman on the **Chicora**. He had worked for the company only a short time and little was known of him except that he was unmarried and had some relatives in Chicago. He was described as, "an affable, accommodating young man, who stood well with his associates."

William Dunn, deckhand

William Dunn, deckhand, was said to have been 38 or 40 years old and a resident of Benton Harbor

John Mattison, deckhand

In some listings John Mattison, 23, of Benton Harbor, is listed as a watchman. The **Chicora**, which he joined in the fall of 1895, was his first lakes experience. He was previously employed at the Oliver plow works in South Bend, Indiana, and had moved to Benton Harbor with Walter Drew, who had obtained a mechanical position in Benton Harbor. One sister, Mrs. Henry Bausley, lived in Benton Harbor.

John Mattison, Deck Hand

Joseph Felix, deckhand

Joseph Felix, deckhand, was estimated to be about 30 years old and resided in Benton Harbor.

Thomas Cass, deckhand

Thomas Cass, deckhand, was estimated to be about 35 years old and was living in Benton Harbor. On some lists the name is given as "Cash."

John Ryan, deckhand

John (some accounts give his first name as Jack) Ryan, deckhand, was estimated to be between 20 and 25 years of age. The newspaper reported, "It is said by his associates that his name was not Ryan but something like Swenski; that he was a Pollander by birth and that he has relatives living in Chicago."

Joseph F. Pearl, passenger

Joseph Franklin Pearl, 31, the only passenger, was a St. Joseph druggist. He was born October 12, 1864, in Benton Township, Berrien County. He graduated from Benton Harbor High School in 1884 and entered the drug store of Geo. M. Bell & Co. in Benton Harbor, working there four years. He graduated from the Chicago School of Pharmacy and in April of 1889 entered into partnership with William Howard in the firm of Howard & Pearl in St. Joseph.

He was married September 11, 1889, to the former May Dempster. The couple had no children. Pearl and his wife had ridden the **Chicora** on the delivery trip from Detroit in 1892. A story in the St. Joseph newspaper said that Pearl had gone on the trip "as a relief from store duty and a slight indisposition."

Pearl was a member of the Masonic lodge of St. Joseph and about two weeks (some accounts say two days) before his death he took out an accident insurance policy for $5,000 with a Masonic organization in Des Moines, Iowa. Because the body was never found the Masonic Mutual Accident Co. at first refused to pay the claim. Mrs. Pearl instituted a suit and in February of 1897, the company settled out of court for $4,000.

Joseph F. Pearl, Passenger

One of the romantic stories to come from the wreck was told by H. B. Spencer and concerns a dog owned by Joseph Pearl. The day the boat left Milwaukee the little dog became uneasy. He would go from one window to another, then sit up in the middle of the room and howl. Mrs. Pearl later spoke of it as a premonition of the disaster.

Although there was no body to bury a memorial stone was created for Joseph Pearl in the Dempster family plot in the old St. Joseph Cemetery.

Mrs. Pearl later married J. W. Mullen, founder of the Mullen Paper Mill of St. Joseph. Her third husband was Joseph Burkhard of St. Joseph. When she died in 1943 she still kept a piece of mahogany trim that had come ashore when the boat went down. It was later given to the Morton Memorial Home in Benton Harbor. Her will also requested that a small designated parcel be buried with her. Friends suspected that it was a bit of the **Chicora** wreckage.

* * *

It was not difficult to name the officers on the **Chicora**. Most of them were well known men and they had actually signed "articles" accepting a position aboard the boat. However, the only record of deck hands and other menial workers was probably in the hands of the clerk aboard the vessel. Since no one was quite certain of even the number of deckhands, oilers and coal passers who went on the last voyage, it is not unlikely that some itinerant sailor, with no friends or family locally to notice that he was missing, might also have been aboard.

Those Who Missed the Boat --

Since there was no official list to guide them, immediately after the disappearance concerned citizens of Benton Harbor and St. Joseph looked around town to see who was missing. Anyone who had not been seen for several days around town was suspected as being on the **Chicora**. Several men were thought to have been on board the boat and their names actually appeared on early lists of the missing but they were later found ashore. One is still included among most lists of victims. These include:

Archibald Bentley, deckhand, about 19, formerly lived with his parents near Bangor, but the father disappeared and the mother died in 1894. He had a 14 year old brother who lived with a farmer east of Bangor and there were said to be other relatives in Cassopolis in Cass County, and near Lake Side, in Berrien County.

"His companions hailed him as a good fellow and his employers always found him attentive to duty."

Both the St. Joseph and Benton Harbor newspaper in their memorial editions added the paragraph, "There is some doubt about Bentley being on board, as parties here claim to have seen him since the wrecking of the boat; but others here believe he was one of the deck hands and we have no reliable information to the contrary."

The February 8 *Three Oaks Press*, carried the note, "Archibald Bentley, whose name appears among the list of **Chicora** lost is employed on Frank Richard's farm near Hersey. Bentley worked as a deck hand on the ill-fated boat last summer but left last fall." In the March 4 issue of the *Benton Harbor Daily Palladium* there is a letter from S. C. Reams of Pipestone who was Archie Bentley's uncle. He reports that his nephew was at Hersey, Michigan, near Reed City, cutting shingle bolts and had been there since November.

Nelson Brundage, better known as "Dot" Brundage, an orphan boy of 17 years of age of Benton Harbor who roomed with Charles Horton, a porter in the Avery block was not on the boat as first reported.

"Ted" Gearing, also supposed to be on the boat, was discovered in jail at Berrien Springs and Horton, who knew all the Bangor boys, told officials and reporters that Gearing's father and two brothers, Matt and Joe, were in Florida, and that none of the Gearings were on the boat.

Patrick Dorahty was at the Gartley House in Benton Harbor the week previous to the sailing of the **Chicora** socializing with other members of the crew, and there was some question about whether he went aboard the boat.

Will Wood was to take that boat, but missed it by five minutes. For many years he sailed the lakes in lumber schooners.

Benjamin Kress of Chicago, formerly of St. Joseph, according to the *Palladium* was in Milwaukee and intended to come across on the **Chicora**. but a hotel clerk neglected to call him in time.

F. J. Lucker of St. Joseph would also have been on the boat had he got to the dock in time when the steamer left Michigan. He was on his way to the dock when the vessel sailed.

Glen Overton of rural Allegan related the story about a sailor from Dowagiac who should have returned to Michigan with the vessel. He was visiting bars in Milwaukee, and became so intoxicated that it wasn't until hours later that he realized he had missed the boat. Believing him lost, bereaved friends in Dowagiac ordered a new cemetery monument and held a funeral. A short time later he walked into town having worked his way home from Milwaukee.

Warren Seabury, a Coloma farmer and fur trader, was scheduled to ride the vessel home after completing business in Milwaukee. He was presumed dead, but a few days later surprised the family by walking in on his own wake. He too had gotten sidetracked in the bars of Milwaukee. This story and the one related by Overton above, might be different versions of the same incident.

Doc Ballinger (spelled Ballingee in some references), an overall manufacturer from St. Joseph, was included in the first list of those missing, as a second passenger aboard. The Benton Harbor newspaper for January 23 noted, "A Chicago paper reports that Doc Ballengee was on the **Chicora**. That is probably a mistake as he is believed to be in Indiana." On January 24, a telegram was received in Benton Harbor from

Ballenger, who was then in Rensselaer, Indiana. "This sets at rest all rumors that he was on board the **Chicora**."

Charles Decker of Bangor was a regular crew member, but he was unable to go on the last trip because of illness.

Arthur Osborn of Benton Harbor regularly served aboard the **Chicora** as second porter. The Benton Harbor paper later reported that Osborn had "intended to go out on the steamer on her fatal trip, but a misunderstanding on his part as to the time she was to leave here kept him at home until too late to get ready to go, thus preserving his life." Because there was just one passenger and a skeleton crew it was probably considered no hardship to sail with only one porter.

William J. Hancock of Saugatuck, the regular clerk of the **Chicora**, was home with his wife who had been ill. He caught the train to St. Joseph but missed the boat when it left for Milwaukee on January 20. As soon as it was determined that the vessel was missing Hancock was put to work as search coordinator. After the loss of the **Chicora** he served on several vessels before becoming clerk on the **City of Milwaukee**. His wife was Caddie Barber, daughter of D. L. Barber who had been a merchant at Saugatuck since 1870. About 1900 he began curtailing his work for Graham & Morton with an eye to staying at home and taking over his father-in-law's store. However, the Barber store and home burned to the ground in November of 1903, and Mrs. Hancock died in January of 1904. Hancock continued to work for Graham & Morton and later remarried.

William Russell, the regular second mate, was sick in bed, but when called he responded that he thought he could make the trip. However, his mother-in-law, who was living with the young couple, was adamant that he remain at home and in bed, and he gave in. When the vessel was reported lost, he was one of the first out on the ice at South Haven. He continued to sail on the Great Lakes and in 1897 was named captain of Graham & Morton's **City of Chicago**. He took time off to recover from the effects of a stroke in 1914, then ended his lakes career working three seasons as wheelsman aboard the **City of St. Joseph**. He retired and lived on for many years. Russell served as an honorary pallbearer at the funeral of J. S. Morton in 1936.

The January 29, 1895 issue of the *Grand Haven Evening News* commented:

> The list of persons who could have been on the **Chicora** during her ill-fated trip had they not overslept, stopped to light a cigar or been subject to some other slight interposition of providence is rapidly increasing. Had they all made proper connections the boat would probably have foundered anyway.

23

Tributes and Memorials

Following the disappearance of the boat the literary output, from amateur and professional poets, was immense. The most famous of the poetic tributes was this poem by Nixon Waterman of the *Chicago Journal*. Waterman was a friend of St. Joseph poet Ben King, who had died in 1893, and served as editor for King's works. The poem Waterman wrote for the **Chicora** owes a lot in rhythm and meter to Edgar Allen Poe's "The Raven." It was recited or sung at all of the memorial ceremonies, reprinted widely in the newspapers of the day, and appears on several of the memorial posters issued following the disaster.

A memorial window in a Benton Harbor store was described in the *Buchanan Record* of January 30, 1895, by the Benton Harbor correspondent:

> Warren's store window has a beautiful memorial of the lost boat and crew. It consists of "Gates Ajar," in pure white against a background of flowers, mostly roses. Just above is a crown of stars, each containing an electric light, the whole surrounded by heavy draperies in black and white. At the bottom a large card, banded with black ribbon contains the words, "Chicora is Lost." It is beautiful, though sad.

There were two major memorial services held in St. Joseph, where organizers said it was impossible to find an auditorium or church big enough to hold all who might want to attend, and a large union service in Benton Harbor.

A memorial service was held at the St. Joseph Congregational church on Sunday, February 10 at 10:30 a.m. to a full house. The only decoration in the sanctuary was a large bouquet of roses and carnations. Special Masonic rites were performed for Captain Stines, James R. Clarke and Joseph Pearl, members of the Knights Templar with all three lodges of the twin cities attending in full uniform and regalia.

The sermon was given by the Rev. H. W. Davis. He said in part:

> We hold today a memorial service for all who went down in that awful storm of January 21st, 1895... With light hearts our friends steamed out into the waters aboard one of the staunchest ships on all the lakes; we loved the craft; she was a part of our common welfare... Our proud and beautiful boat seemed almost conscious of her power; with what grace did she leave our shores and with what majesty did she return, gliding triumphantly into our harbor with her precious human cargoes. She had fought many victorious battles with

A Song and a Sigh

I

Here's a song for the Chicora, for the beautiful Chicora,
  Proudly as a swan she rode the undulating seas --
Dancing o'er the gentle billows, as gracefully as bend the willows.
  Bend the lithe and happy willows to the breath of every breeze.

II

From the bold and busy babble of the city's rush and rabble
  To the fields of fruit and flowers, went she ever to and fro.
Like the seabird floating over the land of soft sweet clover,
  To the bloom-wreathed vales of gladness, to the hills of old St. Joe.

III

O the hearts that watched her going, ever smaller, smaller growing,
  Out upon the seeming shoreless waste of waters, glad and free,
Growing dimmer, dimmer, dimmer, in an iridescent shimmer,
  'Til a speck, she faded between the blue of sky and sea.

IV

Here's a sigh for the Chicora, for the broken, sad Chicora.
  Here's a tear for those who followed her beneath the tossing wave.
O the mystery of the morrow -- from its shadows let us borrow
  A star of hope to shine above the gloom of every grave.

-- Nixon Waterman

wind and wave and we would watch for her and listen for her signals as we would watch for the form and listen for the voice of a friend. . . . her keen prow had cut its way so many times across the lake in calm and storm that we regarded the **Chicora** as invulnerable; but we were mistaken. We did not know the storm's resources -- that there were a thousand furies yet unloosed -- that within cavernous depths were gigantic cauldrons that had never yet sent forth their boiling energies.

The service included "A Man's a Man for a' That" by Scottish poet Robert Burns, recited especially to mark the Masonic friendship of Captain Stines, Clarke and Pearl. A celebration arranged to mark the centennial anniversary of the death of the poet had been canceled by the winter storm and concern over the missing steamer. It concluded with the hymn, "Lead, Kindly Light."

* * *

At the memorial service at the Methodist church in St. Joseph, Waterman's poem, set to music by Arthur Nelson, was sung by Mrs. Kate M. B. Wilson. The Rev. R. H. Bready's sermon said in part:

> Not a season passes that does not bring in a catalogue of wrecked railway trains, foundered boats, storms, accidents; and in this category are even churches struck by lightning, as was illustrated in Benton Harbor a few years ago. It is better that all these things occur than that God's fixed laws be disturbed. These laws were made for man's best good. Suppose every one could have what he thought best, we all have conflicting minds and the earth would be wrecked and in a confusion. . . . Had we been able to have had what we thought best the **Chicora** would not have been wrecked and there would not have been all this sorrow for us to bear. . . .
>
> Fixed laws are made for man's highest good. The Lord alone gives grace and glory, and no good thing will he withhold from those who walk uprightly. When calamities and sorrow come there are no changes in the laws of the universe. If the ill-fated **Chicora** had been loaded with missionaries just returning from Africa or some other foreign country she would have been wrecked just the same.

The service concluded with a choir rendition of, "Jesus Lover of My Soul."

* * *

In Benton Harbor a meeting was held at City Hall to plan a union service to be held at Yore's Opera House Sunday, February 10. More than 1500 mourners squeezed into the building with 50 employees of Graham & Morton marching from the office to the opera house in a body. All of the seats and standing room were "uncomfortably filled," and others stood in the wings of the stage which was trimmed with festoons of black and white gracefully entwined, embellished with rosettes and small flags. A large painting of the **Chicora**, done by Asa Lester, was suspended in front of the proscenium arch and appropriately draped. Most of the clergymen of Benton Harbor had been invited to speak.

The Rev. George A. Sahlin, pastor of the Universalist church spoke for 10 minutes. His remarks were summed up in the local newspaper:

> He said that man is a hero and that woman a heroine who faces duty. In this great shock, the spirit of charity, love and religion has been so well manifested that all regard the calamity as of mutual concern. We accept this sorrow as one of the inevitable occurrences of life. . . . In that supreme hour of peril when the vessel went down all the heroism and fortitude vouchsafed to human beings were called into requisition, but the loved and brave men were unequal to the test and went down to watery graves. They have gone to their eternal life and to us remains the duty of holding up the hands of the living in their hour of trial.

The Rev. W. H. Rice, pastor of the Presbyterian church:

> . . . called attention to this public testimonial as a grand manifestation of public interest. In such times as these universal sympathy is aroused. If money could have brought those men out of their peril no expense would have been deemed extravagant. But neither money, nor skill, nor human entreaty nor effort can cope with the storm king who has held sway over the great lake during the past two weeks. How puny is the arm of man against the elemental forces of nature! . . . In the wreck of the **Chicora** we will ever be ignorant of the circumstances. We may never recover even the forms of those loved ones, but on the hearts of the people of the twin cities are inscribed the words, "Loved, lost, unforgotten."

The Rev. George L. Cady of the Congregational church noted:

> Our lives are closely knit with all the machinery of travel and traffic -- machinery that not only depends upon the brains of living men but the blood of other men sacrificed to its perpetuity. Transportation represents more than mere gold and commercial interest; it reflects the energies of man and the success of human endeavor. . . . If the time ever comes for the sea to give up its dead the speaker had no doubt Robert McClure would be found with his hand upon the throttle of that silent engine, just as he doubtless stood when he went down beneath the waves.

The Rev. J. H. Bicknell, pastor of the Christian church devoted his remarks to words of proffered consolation to the bereaved relatives, spoke of the widespread interest taken in the great disaster and directed all to God for comfort.

The Rev. Robert Miller of Second Baptist (colored) church:

> ... spoke feelingly of the lost **Chicora**, gone down with her gallant company of human souls. Our lease of life is short at best and will be but a comparatively short time when we shall follow those who have gone before. He counseled all to raise their eyes about the trials and vicissitudes of life to the happiness and rewards and glory that is promised to those who rightly meet the duties of life.

The service also included a cornet dirge with piano accompaniment played by Fred H. Null and Mrs. F. B. Christopher, a solo "Anchored," by Mr. Christopher, and a collection to defray expenses of the service. It closed with one verse of "Rock of Ages."

* * *

In addition to the Waterman poem printed above, the memorial newspaper issued by the St. Joseph newspaper carried the following poem by a city resident:

In Memorium
Jan. 25, 1895

With ice beleaguered, with mad winds tossed --
While furious waves their pathway crossed
    And gathering tempests roared;
Through storm-dark clouds there gleamed a light
That reached from heaven's hallowed height
    To each brave heart on board.

And through the radiant rifts on high
Was heard "Ahoy!" 'twas God's own cry
    Amid the blinding foam;
And back each breast its answer gave,
Beseeching that His mercies save
    And shield the loved at home.

No craven wish made manhood cower
To dim its lustre in that hour
    As high the seething spray
Swept o'er the ship, each stoutly bore
A motto, though the wild waves tore,
    Of "God and home for aye."

As heaven's immortal gates were swung,
An anthem from an angel's tongue
    Was heard above the blast;
Singing a requiem o'er the dead --

Placing a wreath upon each head
    Whose thoughts of home were last.

Blow gently, winds, a lulling air,
Wash lightly, waves, those bosoms there.
    Their sad'ning work is done;
And though thou mayest of life bereft,
That fond, enduring love is left
    That lives when life is gone.

                J. S. Schuler

The newspaper in Benton Harbor, not to be outdone, printed two new memorial poems in its January 29 edition:

The Lost Chicora

O, winds that drive to madness the waters of the deep,
Blow gently to our sorrowing hearts, and tell where loved ones sleep.
Tell of the storm and waves that washed our vessel to and fro;
And how brave souls withstood the blasts and hurricane of woe.

O, winds that wail o'er troubled deeps, forbear forbear to rave,
Lest thou disturb the silence of a deep, unfathomed grave,
Bear down on wings like dove let loose with olive branch of peace;
And give to weeping souls now rent the balm of sweet release.

O, winds relentless, cease your strife and sleep in calm repose;
Give peace to wave-washed ones that rest, and hope to hearts of those
Who waited, watched the heaving swells for tidings of the lost,
As wave on wave came rolling o'er, by raging tempest tossed.

O, winds of life! O, boisterous wave! broad ocean full of grief;
How oft, alas! our bark goes down while praying for relief,
How oft as morning suns arise to welcome a new day,
Do storms forecast and waves break o'er before is full mid-day.

O, winds of heaven blow calm and still, bequeath to weeping shore,
The voice of hope from realms beyond, and peace for evermore.
Dispel the gloom of cloud and storm, however dark and rife;
And give release to sorrowing ones and joy of restful life.

                by Frances Browning Owen

The Brave Dead

(Written for the *Palladium*)

The storm wind with angry roar,
Beat strong against the ice-bound shore;
With driving sleet of snow and hail,
That blanched the bravest seaman pale;
Which drove before its chilling blast,
With headlong speed so furious fast,
Into those mountain peaks of ice,
That crushed it like a Titan's vice;
The great **Chicora** strong and brave,
Rushed on impelled by wind and wave;
Into those icebergs rising high,
That force of wind and wave defy;
Rushed on to where no hand could save,
And gave her crew a watery grave.
That awful scene what brush or pen
Can paint or tell us of those men?
Brave men who never knew a fear,
To duty true though death be near;
Brave men who saw the distant shore,
And thought of homes they'd see no more;
Brave men in freezing tempest tossed,
They knew and felt that all was lost;
Who when those icy decks they trod,
With helpless souls looked up to God
In prayer that only God could hear,
(Tho' fierce the storm, God's ever near)
Drenched chilled, benumbed by icy wave,
In earnest prayer their souls to save;
And though beneath the waves they sleep,
Where wintry winds their vigil keep;
Those prayers were heard and answer given.
Their souls are anchored safe in heaven.

J. L. Anderson
Battle Creek, Michigan, Jan. 26

* * *

Several other newspapers printed memorial poems written by their readers. The *Grand Haven Evening News* of January 28, 1895, featured "Wreck of the Chicora." The author is given as "Babe," and further described as, "a young man of Grand Haven."

Wreck of the Chicora

Yea, on that fatal winter's eve
The **Chicora** from her port took leave,
Unconscious of the threatening storm,
Her sides on which it must be borne.

As on each wave she rose and fell
The Captain took the course known well
And through the midnight dark and drear,
She plunged into the storm so near!

All night she sped on through the blast,
Which came like fire from Hades at last,
Each sailor stood at duty's post,
As the snow swept down in blinding hosts.

God bless them who outside had stayed
And watched in sore despair each wave,
And for the breaking of the morn,
For which each heart beat sad, forlorn.

And when along the frozen shore
The party found some wreck and doors,
The truth at once then to them came
Of how the crew had went the same.

And how each man had tried to save,
The ship and all from such a grave,
But in the strife to reach the shore
Each sank to sleep forever more.

by Babe

* * *

Some tributes have not survived. In the *Saugatuck Commercial* for March 1, 1895, the editor wrote:

> Every great marine disaster on the lakes is certain sooner or later to be memorized in song. The latest of these ballads is entitled, "The Fate of the Chicora" and its first public rendering was at the Musical entertainment last Saturday evening when it was sung with good effect by Mrs. G. W. Babcock. The words and music of this song are by Mrs. Bessie Mitchell who formerly resided here, and is a testimony of her gift and skill as a composer.

The *Three Oaks Press* describes a song entitled "The Ill-Fated Chicora" composed by W. C. Dobey of Chicago and set to music by Frank D. Smith of Chicago, formerly of Benton Harbor. The title page shows a vessel laboring in an angry sea and covered with ice, "being an idealization of the supposed fate of the lost steamer."

* * *

The broken off spars of the **Chicora** had been discovered ashore on the ice not far from the Village of Douglas, south of the Kalamazoo River, south of Saugatuck. The *Douglas Weekly Record* reported the first part of February that "President Wade wired the Graham Transportation Co., at St. Joseph, asking for the donation of the spars of the ill-fated **Chicora**, and received a response granting the request. One of the sticks, 57 feet in length, has already been secured and a gang of men are now on the ice after the other one. Carpenters will at once join the two pieces and make a shapely pole, and it will be erected at the corner of Center and Union Streets." Wade was president of the Village of Douglas.

The two spars were hauled ashore, some of the area newspapers wrote in scorn "after an almost endless amount of labor" and the flagstaff completed. It was dedicated the last of February. The March 1, 1895, *Saugatuck Commercial* reported, "The new flag staff at Douglas made from the spars of the steamer **Chicora** was raised last Monday in the presence of a number of people. A short address was made by Rev. Mr. Peatling and the band played some patriotic airs. The new pole is ninety-five feet high, is surmounted by a model of the Chicora designed by Wm. Shashaguay and is provided with a flag thirty-six feet long."

The *Holland City News* added, ". . . aside from its ornamental features the pole will have much value as an historical monument of one of the great marine disasters of Lake Michigan."

The flag staff was erected at the corner of Center and Union Streets on the northeast corner of the large white building which was shared by the Village of Douglas and the Dutcher Masonic lodge. It was used for many years but fell victim to both wood rot and a street widening project. The remains of the flag staff were hauled off to an Allegan county dump.

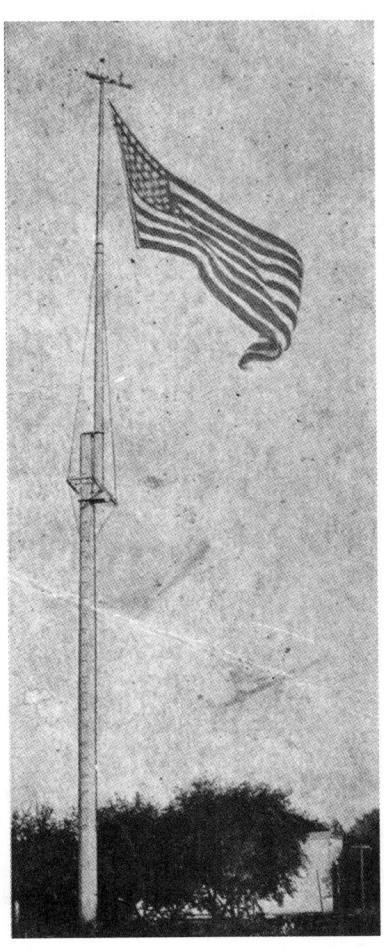

The Douglas flagpole

In 1963 the Allegan County Historical Society began planning a museum to be built in the old jail. The son of a former Fennville postmaster, "Nick" Carter told members that he knew where the mast of the **Chicora** was and led them to a spot near the side of the dump where the top portion of the flagpole, with the flag pulley still attached, lay on the ground. Society members cut off a small portion of the bottom which was badly rotted and took a 30-foot section by truck to Allegan. The tall pole was installed in the cellblock stairwell of the old jail. The tip is encircled by several iron bands and there is a wooden peg at the top that probably held the carved boat, and might earlier have secured the traditional gilded ball at the top of the mast.

The Allegan museum collection also includes the purser's box which was discovered in the sand near Saugatuck, the brass lock mechanism from the pilothouse door which came ashore near what was later the Allegan County West Side Park, and a half-rounded piece of timber that was said to be part of the **Chicora** wreckage.

The Shashaguay family, of Indian descent, appear on the 1840 Saugatuck Township census. Joseph Shashaguay later carved a number of full models of the **Chicora** and some bas relief plaques for exhibit and sale.

The remains of the mast photographed from the first floor (right) and from the second floor (left) showing the tip. The timber at left is also said to be from the Chicora.

Irving K. Pershing, a columnist for Saugatuck's *Commercial Record*, wrote in 1993 that when the masts came ashore the ship's bell was still attached to one of them. This bell was retrieved by a Douglas resident and for many years functioned as the fire bell, mounted outside the old telephone exchange in downtown Douglas. When it was replaced by a new fire siren, Pershing asked for the old bronze bell and had it mounted on a steel carriage with wooden wheels, for the use of the whole community for parades and other celebrations. The bell was later lent out for use during a party and not returned.

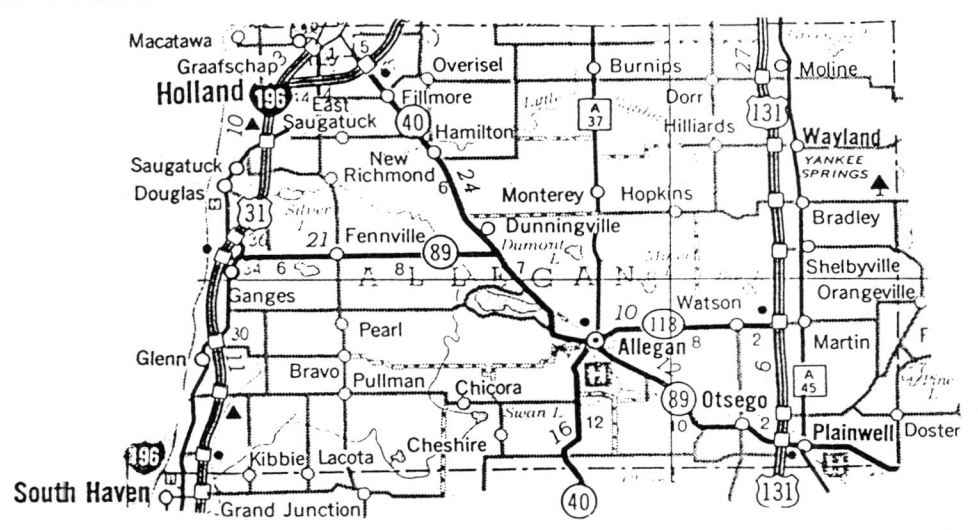

Although the post office closed in 1904 the settlement of Chicora (bottom center) continues on state highway maps of Allegan County.

The Chicora post office which opened January 10, 1896, in Cheshire Township, in southeastern Allegan county, was named for the lost ship by its first postmaster Herman D. Clark. The story at the time was that residents were split over what to call the little settlement. It had always been referred to simply as "The Corners" but a more formal name was needed. One side wanted Troopville, the other almost anything else. An elderly lady suggested honoring the **Chicora** and the compromise was accepted. The office was short lived operating only until May 31, 1904, a time when many small post offices were replaced by rural free delivery. On the back wall of the Giles general store on 108th Avenue a display for many years depicted the tragic story of the town's namesake. It was removed by Basil Giles when the store was sold before 1957. The same, or a similar, memorial poster with crumbling gilded frame now hangs in the Allegan County Museum with other **Chicora** memorabilia.

* * *

For many years a piece of shattered wood from the lost steamer was displayed above the counter of Griffin's drug store in Niles.

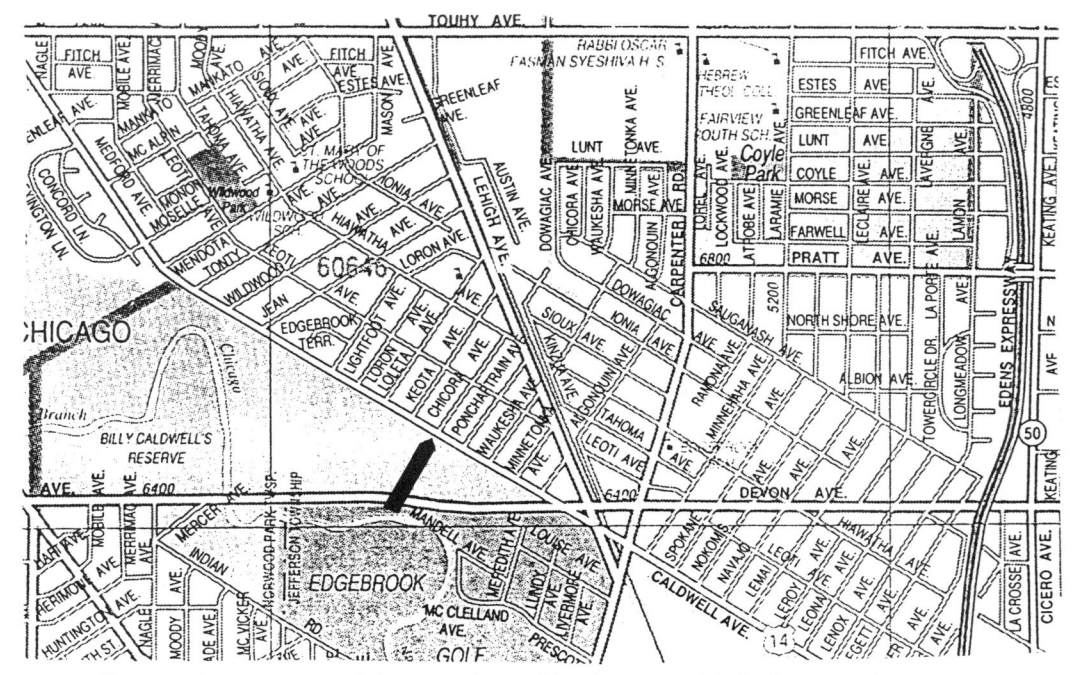

Chicora Avenue (arrow) is part of a series of streets with Indian sounding names.

Chicora Avenue, a north-south street in the northwest corner of Chicago was named for the wrecked boat. It is located just north of the Edgebrook Golf Course.

* * *

At the Josephine Morton Memorial Home, 501 Territorial Road, Benton Harbor, the ancestral home of J. S. Morton, a special exhibit in 1986 included a chair from the **Chicora** (part of the furniture already in storage before the final trip), and a painting of the vessel from the 1839 Courthouse Museum, Berrien Springs.

The Josephine Morton Memorial Home in Benton Harbor

Although there was discussion in the newspapers following the disaster advocating a memorial stone, one was never erected. The event is remembered in stone only on the memorial marker for passenger Joseph F. Pearl near the entrance of the old St. Joseph Cemetery on Lakeside Street. The memorial is in the Dempster plot, the family of his wife. At the base of a tall stone, with an urn-shaped paramount, the last verse of the Waterman poem, beginning "Here's a sigh for the **Chicora**. . ." is engraved.

The stone in the Dempster plot of the old St. Joseph cemetery. The tall marker has a memorial to Joseph F. Pearl at right, with the last verse from the Waterman poem inscribed on the base of the stone below.

The Graham & Morton Transportation Co. still had its best years ahead. At the end of February, 1895, the **Petoskey** was finally freed from her icy prison and began making regular trips to Milwaukee until the company's charter of her ended in April. The first week of April the **R. C. Reid** was finished at the dry docks. She had been lengthened nearly 50 feet and her tonnage had been increased from 332 gross tons to 554 gross tons and her net tonnage nearly doubled from 214 to 451. At her relaunch

147

in April, 1895, she received a new name, **City of Louisville.** As a third boat Graham & Morton leased and then purchased the 245 foot, 1,148 ton vessel **City of Milwaukee** which had been built for the Goodrich Line in 1881.

According to the minutes of the January 14, 1896, meeting of Graham & Morton stockholders, the company eventually paid at least $15,000 to the Big Four railway as compensation for the lost cargo of flour. The report stated in part, "While the company was not legally liable for the loss, yet the Directors of the Company felt that the claims on this account should be paid." Cargo for the Big Four railway continued to be an important part of Graham & Morton's cargo business.

The Graham & Morton company purchased additional steamboats and began to serve other cities eventually running direct boats from Holland, Saugatuck and South Haven to Chicago. Business appeared to be at a peak during the season of 1924. This all ended when the City of Chicago announced its intention to rebuild the dock area downtown. Graham & Morton owned space in Chicago on the south bank of the Chicago river extending west from the Rush Street bridge to Dearborn Street. Vessels using it had to negotiate a minimum of bridges and were very near the South Water Market. But by 1924 the city needed the land to complete a waterfront project and G & M no longer had a stopping place in Chicago. This, and a number of financial considerations, prompted a merger with the Goodrich Transit Co. in mid-October of 1924.

Dwindling freight traffic as a result of the competition of motorized carriers and a generally poor economic picture spelled the doom of large-volume lake traffic. Goodrich Transit filed a voluntary bankruptcy petition December 20, 1932.

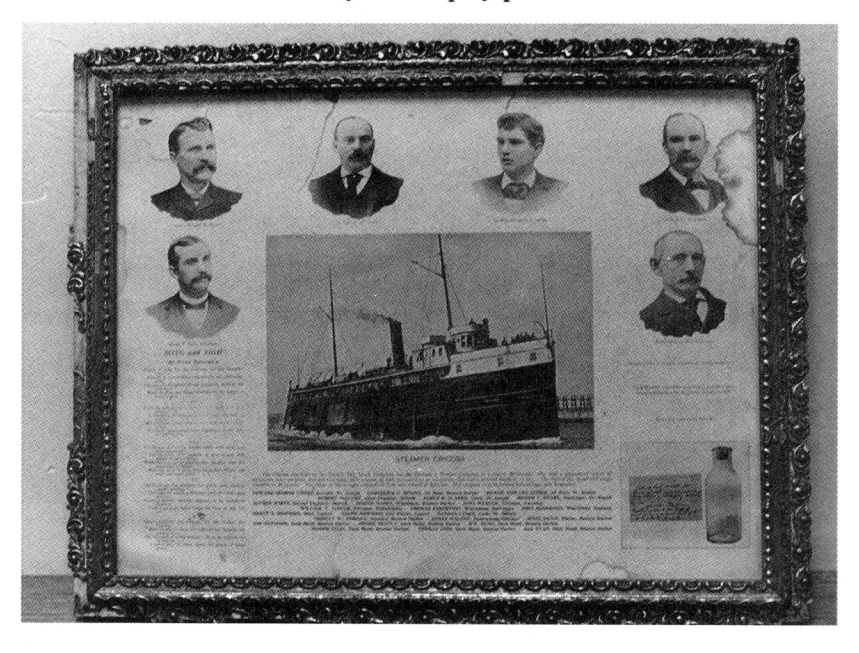

A framed memorial poster in the Allegan museum. Larger posters are located in western Michigan at the Tri-Cities Museum in Grand Haven and the Michigan Maritime Museum in South Haven.

24

The Search Continues

The first week of November, 1895, additional wreckage was blown into St. Joseph following a storm and the *South Haven Messenger* for November 22, 1895, carried the terse note, "Graham & Morton announce that they will commence searching for the wreck of the **Chicora** the first calm day. It is thought she is within a radius of eight miles to the south." But there is no evidence that an intensive search was made at this time.

* * *

Many different methods were attempted including the supernatural. The *South Haven Sentinel* reported, September 25, 1896:

> A dispatch, the substance being as though it came from an unknown world, but which for the benefit of the ordinary frail mortal is dated at Benton Harbor, Monday, says: Prof. James Gustin, a spiritualist, who has been here several weeks attempting to locate the lost steamer **Chicora**, announced today that he has located it in the lake ten miles out and 255 1/2 feet from the lighthouse at St. Joseph in 180 feet of water. He presented a document at the Graham & Morton offices in this city this afternoon which he says was signed by Capt. Edward Stines and Clerk Jas. R. Clarke of the lost steamer, and Dr. S. B. Ellsworth, a spiritualist of this city. In the document, which is an agreement between Prof. Gustin and the crew of the boat, the professor agrees with the dead to divide the reward of $10,000, provided the departed locate the boat. The document names amounts from $2,000 down for the relatives of each member of the crew. Prof. Gustin claims he has accomplished all of his business with Mr. Clarke, the clerk, and that he talked with him the last time Sunday night.

* * *

The June 11, 1897, issue of the *Saugatuck Commercial* reported that "A wreck was located 12 miles off of St. Joseph by the fishing tug **Sir Arthur**. They found a 40 foot long black spar attached to something on the bottom." It could not be relocated.

* * *

In September of 1898, Captain Edward Napier approached Graham & Morton with a proposal to locate the wreck, according to the *South Haven Sentinel* of September 2, 1898:

> Capt. Napier, as well as many well posted marine men, think the wreck can be located, if the work is carried out in a systematic way, according to the plans of the present searchers. With a careful study of every condition of the lost boat -- the weather, velocity of the wind at various times, the speed of the boat and where the first wreckage was discovered. Capt. Napier has based his idea as to just in what territory the lost boat can be found. He has stated he is sure the wreck lies southwest of South Haven; that the **Chicora** was making for St. Joseph when she became disabled in a blinding snow storm, gradually worked toward the shore and without power got caught in the trough of the sea and went down. He also stated the well established fact that wreckage below forty feet of water never rises, as did the wreckage from the **Chicora**, and therefore she must be near shore in shallow water.

On September 17 the tug **George B. McClellan** arrived in St. Joseph and the following week the paper carried the news that Captain Napier was getting ready to move to St. Joseph. However, a note in the September 17, *South Haven Sentinel* reported "He is unable to make satisfactory arrangements with the Graham & Morton Company about the percentage of salvage, and this may cause some delay." The following week, on October 1, the Benton Harbor newspaper carried the brief notice, "Capt. Ed. Napier will not search for the lost **Chicora**. He has left for Michigan City with his tug to engage in the towing business."

* * *

In August of 1901, Captain Joe Smith of the steamer **R. J. Gordon**, thought that he had found the **Chicora**. He was headed to St. Joseph August 19 with a boat load of excursionists from South Haven when he spotted a spar sticking about a foot out of the water 12 or 19 miles on the St. Joseph-South Haven course and between a half and 3/4 mile from shore. "He noticed that the spar was stationary as the waves washing over it did not move it." It took him two tries to relocate the object, and he took ropes to fasten on to it and returned to port with a pond net pole, 40 feet in length and from six to ten inches in diameter.

* * *

In 1901 there was another attempt to locate the vessel with help from the spirit world. The *Benton Harbor Palladium* reported, August 16, 1901:

> Mrs. Sarah E. Bromwell, the Chicago spiritual medium is here again to resume her search for the **Chicora**. She believes the lost boat will be found within a few days.

Mrs. Bromwell has employed a submarine diver, whose brother died recently and sent a message from the spirit world to Mrs. Bromwell telling her of the location of the lost ship. This diver will aid in the search. Will Moyer's boat will be used to take the diver and his apparatus out in the lake.

Mrs. Bromwell has a rival, a Mrs. Robinson, from Elkhart, who says she intends to find the boat. Both the deluded ladies seem to be in earnest in their pursuit of the phantom ship.

Mrs. Bromwell is accompanied by members of the "Sunlight Center Club" of Chicago who profess faith in her ability to carry out her project.

According to news stories Mrs. Bromwell began her work shortly after the boat went down, searching for a medium to speak to the proper spirits. When she arrived in Benton Harbor September 12, she had engaged the services of a certain diver recommended to her by a spirit and perfected an electric arrangement that was expected to locate the wreck when the electric launch hired for the search arrived in the correct area. The *South Haven Daily Tribune* for September 13, noted, "The doings of this woman are watched with a great deal of interest as she is a truly remarkable faculty and is at least honest in her convictions that she will at last located the boat."

However bad weather made it difficult for a boat, and impossible for a diver and by September 18, Mrs. Bromwell had returned to Chicago. The *Benton Harbor News* said: "The severe weather of the past few days has made the search impracticable and it is doubtful whether she will ever resume it."

* * *

In the middle 1970's fishing boats from the Saugatuck area brought up what appears to be a section of stern from a wooden vessel that was one and a half feet wide and five feet long, weighing more than 200 pounds. It showed the curvature of the stern and appeared to be the base of a railing. An area marine historian who inspected the artifact reported that there were flecks of bright green and yellow paint still clinging to it, colors known to have been used by Graham & Morton. Also that the weight and thickness of the section could have been from a wooden steamer about the size of the **Chicora**. The find was brought up near a reef of rocks located in Lake Michigan, south of Saugatuck near Pier Cove. If the area has been further explored no reports have been filed with authorities.

* * *

In 1987 Charles Sizelove, an employee of Breakwater Marine Salvage of Kalamazoo, announced that he had located the **Chicora** and Louis Wayne Simpson, owner of the company applied to the state Department of Natural Resources for permits to salvage the wreck. According to a story in the December 30, 1987, issue of the *Herald-Palladium* Simpson said that he had actually been on the ship, but that the company would not disclose the location of the vessel or release any information about the find until permits were approved.

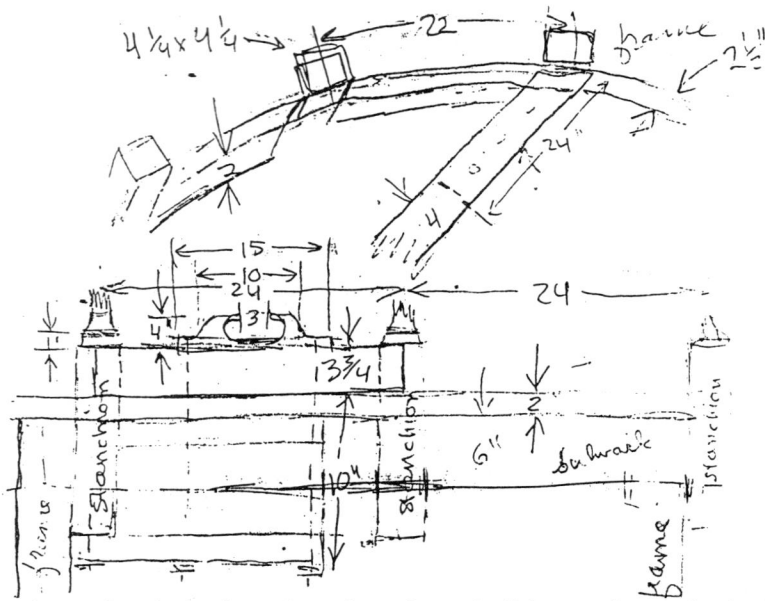

Two views of a piece of wreckage brought up in fisherman's nets in the 1970's.

The Michigan Department of Natural Resources refused to issue the permit without the location on the application. One Michigan diver who assisted with the evaluation by the DNR said that the department was not convinced that Breakwater Marine actually knew the location of the **Chicora**. It appeared, he said, that Breakwater had made a prior agreement with a company which had a sonar device and would only participate in the project if the salvage permit was in hand before they started.

* * *

The Southwest Michigan Underwater Preserve under consideration for the east shore of Lake Michigan New Buffalo to Holland is seen as offering some protection if it is implemented. In providing documentation to accompany the application a side-scan sonar was made of the area. "The survey included the area where the **Chicora** is expected to be," according to Ken Pott of the Michigan Maritime Museum, South Haven, who is assisting with the application process. "We identified several anomalous irregularities on the bottom that could be natural or might be the remains of a vessel, but there wasn't one that leaps out and screams **Chicora**." In addition to providing on-the-spot radar-type pictures the device also recorded the configuration of the bottom for future use.

"One of the problems is that we are not sure what the **Chicora** would look like," Pott said. "We don't known whether it would be in one piece, or two, or several. Whether it is on its side or back. If the vessel is in shallow water it would be broken up over time and cover a large area." He said he does expect that one day it will be found and identified.

Some divers hint that the resting place of the hull of the **Chicora** has already been found but its location has not been divulged for fear that the wreck will be scavenged. To date the disappearance of the **Chicora** remains a mystery.

Index

Agnew, J. K. V. 81
Alden Canning Co. 6,9
Allegan 96,113,114,144
Allegan County Historical
  Society 113,144,148
Allegan Gazette 66,113
Alpena 122
Alpena 1,42
Anderson, J. L. 141
Ann Arbor No. 1 32
Ann Arbor RR 6
Archer the florist, 18
Arden 105
Armstrong, Paul 93
Avery, Mr. 101,102
Avery, Mrs. H. M. 101

Babcock, Mrs. G. W. 142
"Babe" 141-42
Baintridge Twp. 125
Balch, C. M. 111
Ballenger, Doc 26,91,133-34
Baltimore & Ohio 84
Baltimore, Md. 125
Bangor 16,99,132
Bangor Advance 92
Barber, D. L. 64,134
Barnes, Burdette C. 9
Barnes, Jessie C. (Crawford) 9
Barry, Edward 31
Barry, Thomas 67-68
Bartram, Miss 19
Bausley, Mrs. Henry 130
Baxter, Sarah Louise 7
Beeson's Marine Directory 15
Bell, Geo. M. & Co. 131
Belle Chase 116
Belle of the Lake 129
Beloit, Wis. 30
Bentley, Archibald 132
Bentley, Fred 52
Benton Harbor 1,6-13,18,20,
  21,25-27,31,38,40,42,43,47,
  48,50,54,58,64,67,70,79,86,
  89,90,96,101,106-108,117,
  122,125-136,143,146,149,150
Benton Harbor & St. Joseph
  Gas and Fuel Co. 9
*Benton Harbor Banner
  -Register* 121
*Benton Harbor Daily
Palladium* 1,10,23,25,28,
  38,39,42,43,46,47,52,54,
  56,63,64,66,68,69,77,78,
  81,85,88,90,92,98,101,
  107,112,118,121,141,150
Benton Harbor Evening News
  10,151
*Benton Harbor News
  -Palladium* 10
Benton Harbor Improvement
  Co. 9
Benton Harbor Woman's
  Club 11
Berrien 13
Berrien Springs 133
Berrien Springs Journal Era
  57,63,108
Bicknell, Rev. J. H. 138
Big Four RR 18,23,24,25,
  30,56,58,81,148
Bjork, Oscar 58
Blodgett Milling Co. 30
Blow, Lt. 44
Bluffington, Ind. 123
Boone Co., Ill. 6
Bostick, Dr. 98
Bowman, Mrs. and Mrs.
  Charles 19
Boyne, Capt. John 42,43,52
Bradley, Carl D. 1
Bradshaw, Mabel 122,125
Brammel, E. 106
"The Brave Dead" 141
Bready, R. H. 137
Breakwater Marine Salvage
  151-52
Brimmer, Carl 116
Brimmer, Henry 116
Brittain, R. C. 64,69
Bromley, W. W. 73
Bromwell, Mrs. Sarah E.
  150-51
Brooklyn, NY 129
Brundage, Nelson "Dot" 133
Brunson, Sterne 11
Bryant Manufacturing Co.
  120
Buchanan Record 1,98,108,
  135
Bundy, W. N. 98
Burkenhead, England 15
Burkhard, Joseph 132
Burns, Edward 90
Burns, Robert 137

Cadwell, E. W. 46
Cady, George L. 138
Calumet 86-88
Calvert, T. P. 86
Campbell, Walter K. 4
Carter, "Nick" 144
Carthage, Ind. 127
Casco Twp. 39,41,104
Cass (or Cash), Thomas 131
Cassopolis 132
Cayuga 16
Charleston, S.C. 15
Chase, Dora E. 7
Chesebro, Allen 45,101,102,
  103,120
Chicago, Ill. 6,8-11,13,17,18,
  20,23,28,30,31,36-39,42,44,
  48,51,56,63,67,68,75,78,79,
  94,125,129,130,133,143,146,
  148,150,151
Chicago 81
Chicago and West Michigan
  RR 81
Chicago InterOcean 33,44,51,
  67,68,72,83,90,91
Chicago Journal 135
Chicago Herald 68
Chicago Record 79
Chicago Times Herald 37-38,
Chicago Tribune 31,35,37,42,
  43,53,54,55,56,81,83,86,87,88
Chicora (1864) 15,16
Chicora Company 15
Chippewa 16
Christopher, Mr. and Mrs.
  F. B. 139
Cibola 16
City of Chicago 13,18,23,46,
  58,101,107,121,122,124,134
City of Grand Rapids 11,58
City of Milwaukee 134,148
City of Louisville 148
City of Ludington 36,44,73-
  76,126
City of St. Joseph 13,134
Clark, Herman D. 145
Clarke, James R. 26,29,30,50,
  53,124,135,137,149
Clarke, Alethia H.
  (Goodrich) 124
Clarke, Mrs. 46
Clements Mr. 113
Cleveland, Ohio 18,126

153

Cleveland, Cincinnati, Chicago and St. Louis Rwy. 23 (also see Big Four)
Cochrane, Capt. 29
Coleridge, Samuel T. 29
Coloma 57,133
Commercial Record 99,145
Conger, Alta 19
Consaul, Capt. Henry 86-87
Corona 16,126
Covert 99
Craithie 74
Crawford, Andrew 6,7,9,11, 36,37,38,48,50,83
Crawford, Andrew H. 9
Crawford, Richard C. 9
Crawford Transportation Co. 9
Crosby 48
Crosby, Ida L. 130
Curran, Andy 45
Cutler, Solon 57

Daily Calumet 84,88,91
Davenport, A. J. 83
Davis, Austin B. 127
Davis, Elisha 127
Davis, Rev. H. W. 53,135
Davis, Hawley 127
Davis, J. L. 84
Davis, Jesse C. 126-27
Davis, Florence (Robinson) 127
Decker, Charles 26,134
Democrat, The 70
Dempster, Mrs. 19
Dempster, May 131
Detroit 15,16,18,25,26,36,46, 54,72,94,127,128
Detroit, Belle Isle and Windsor Ferry Co. 4
Detroit Drydock Co. 13,14,21
Detroit Evening News 92
Detroit Free Press 4,16,32,36, 43,54,57,72,94,111
Detroit Journal 65
Detroit Tribune 25
Diamond 116
Dickinson, William 67-68,70
Dix, John A. 29
Dionne, Capt. Edward 86-88
Dobey, W. D. 143
Donahue, Charles 40,117,118
Dorahty, Patrick 133
Douglas 62,63,112,143,145
Douglas Weekly Record 143

Downer, Rosel 96
Downing, Grant 26,129
Downing, Ralph 26,129
Doyle, Frank 90
Drew, Walter 130
Dunham, J. S. 37,88,90
Dunham Towing and Wrecking Co. 37,38,63,90
Durham, Charles 69
Dunn, William 130

Eastland 1
Edward, Frank 96
Elbe 74
Elkhart, Ind. 6,151
Ellsworth, S. B. 149
Elphicke, C. W. 82
Estee, T. C. 30
Evening Wisconsin 77,78,94
Excelsior Gas Co. 9
F. & P.M. No. 1 114
F. & P.M. No. 4 34
Farmington, George 48
"The Fate of the Chicora" 142
Felix, Joseph 131
Fenton, Michael 86
Fifield, Mayor 86
First National Bank of Benton Harbor 9
Fitzgerald, Edmund 1
Frankfort 32,39
French, L. 86
Fullriede, Margaret (Umphrey) 57

Ganges Twp 104,118
Gard, Mr. and Mrs. John F. 18
Gearing, Joe 133
Gearing, Matt 133
Gearing, Ted 133
Geneseo, Ill. 7,8
Giles, Basil 145
Glen Haven 52
Glencoe, Ill. 110
Glenn 101,104,106
Goodrich, Alethia H. 124
Goodrich, Solon S. 129
Goodrich Transit Co. 11,13, 73,124,148
Gordon, R. J. 150
Goss, Henry R. 99-100
Graham & Morton & Co. 11
Graham, John 6
Graham, John H. 6-9,11,13,18,26,31,34-37,41,43,

47,50,54,56,57,61,63,67,70, 73,75,77-79,81,86,90,94,107, 108,128
Graham, Lucinda (Nichols) 6
Graham, Mrs. E. A. 18
Graham, May 18
Grand Haven 31,73-75,97,141
Grand Haven Evening News 57-58,141
Grand Haven Evening Tribune 48,111
Grand Junction 43
Grand Rapids 54,122,124
Grand Rapids Democrat 66,77
Graves, Frank P. 9
Graves, Lucy (Crawford) 9
Grice & Gays 113
Griffin 1
Griffin, Captain John 26,43,56,77,78
Guide 121
Gustin, James 149

Halliday 82
Hagar 98
Hammond, Ind. 92
Hancock, Caddie (Barber) 26
Hancock, William J. 18,21,26, 43,47,51,52,54,61,64,66, 69,70,90,91,107,113,134
Hancock, Caddie (Barber) 134
Hare, William 101
Harmon, O. E. 43
Hartford 125,126
Harvey, George 96
Hausler, M. 82
Heath, Carrie 10
Heath, E. W. 67
Heath, H. F. 85,88
Herbert 120
Hersey 132,133
Hiar, William 101
Higgins, E. 86
Hinsdale, Ill. 11
History of Michigan 9
Hirner, Herman 112
Hobbs, Fred A. 49,50
Hogarth, Jack 86
Hogeboom, Ida (Crosby) 130
Hogeboom, John G. 129-30
Holland 26,35,42,114,148,152
Holland City News 37,143
Holland, Saugatuck & Southeastern RR 96
Homer 7

154

Hopkins, Fred 19
Hopkins, Martin 52
Horton, Charles 133
Howard & Pearl 53,108,131
Howe, M. A. 99
Hull, Charles 11
Hummel, Ernest 84
Humiston, G. A. 116
Hummiston, George 46

Hyde Park, Ill. 86

"I Fed the Fishes" 21
"The Ill-Fated Chicora" 143
"In Memorium" 139
Independent Towing Co. 67
Indiana 13,16
Indianapolis, Ind. 23

Jacksonville, Fla. 125
Jedlicka, George 120
Jedlicka, Jerry 120
Jenkins, Capt. W. H. 84
Jewel, George 90
Johnson Bros. 116

Kalamazoo 54,129
Kalamazoo Daily Telegraph 51,52,55,59,111
Kalamazoo Evening News 56
Keeler & Hogeboom 130
Keeler, William 130
Kern, B. & Sons 30
Kewaunee 39
Kibbie 104
Kime, Tom 45
Kimsey, W. T. 99
King, Ben 21,135
Kingsland, Margaret 18
Kirby 16
Kirby, Frank E. 13,16, 19-20
Klein, P. J. 77
Kohl & Middleton 57
Kress, Benjamin 133

LaCrosse, Wis. 30
Lakeside 132
Lapeer 129
Lawrence 96
Lewach, Mrs. A. D. 102
Leggett, George E. 18
Lessor, John 120
Lester, Asa 138
Let Her Be 15
Lincoln Park 8,38,83
Listmann Milling Co. 30
Little Sable Pt. 37,44

London, Ont. 123
Lora 13,17,23,121,124
"The Lost Chicora" 140
Lucker, F. J. 133
Ludington 31.34.37.39,73,122
Ludington (see **City of Ludington**)
Lull, R. 52
Lynch, Nathan R. 126
Lynch, Sarah 126

Macatawa 42
Makin, F. A. 96-97
Malone, James E. 26
Malone, James 130
Manistee 23,31,77,78,115
Manistee Advocate 77-78
Manistee Daily News 78
Manitowoc, Wis. 73
Manitou Islands 39,52,93
Mankato, Minn. 30
Mann Bros. 30
Mann, Levi 18
"A Man's a Man for a' That" 137
Marks, Joseph 123-24
Matthews, Capt. Lew 40,43,50,51,52,59
Mattison, John 130
Maxwell 122
McAnte, Engineer 98
McAvoy, Jonathan 67
McClellan, George B. 150
McClure, Charles F. 127
McClure, George R. 127
McClure, Harold E. 108 -110,127
McClure, Herbert V. 127
McClure, J. D. 106
McClure, James 117
McClure, Robert 18,26,46,50, 101,106,107,108.109.110, 114,117,127
McClure, Robert C. 127
McClure, William J. 46,101, 108,117,127
McCormick, James 67
McDermott, Mechanic 84
McIntosh, Angus 124
McLure 107,108
McNamara, Sgt. 84
Meaford, Ont. 124
Menier, Fred 96
Menominee 32
Messenger 13,121
Metropolis 127
Michigan City 44,48,98-99, 116
Michigan City Dispatch 28, 117
Michigan City News 91,96,98, 107,114,115,117,120
Michigan Dept. of Natural Resources 152
Michigan Maritime Museum 148,152
Miller, William 26
Miller, William C. & Son 15
Miller, Rev. Robert 139
Miller's Station, Ind. 85,90
Milsted, Daisy (Crawford) 9
Milsted, T. G. 9
Milwaukee, Wis. 6,17,20,25, 26,28,30-34,36,43,44,50,56, 73,75,77,93,126,133
Milwaukee Malt & Grain Co. 30
Milwaukee Sentinel 28,30
Miner, Frank 86
Minneapolis, Minn. 30,129
Mitchel, Mrs. Della 125
Mitchell, Mrs. Bessie 142
Mollhagen & Co. 120
Mollhagen, Charles 120
Montreal, Que. 15,124
Moore, Charles 9
Moore, Professor 38
Morford, T. T. 25,28,90,91
Morgan, Charles 126
Morgan, Chloe 126
Morgan, Edwin 126
Morgan, George 126
Morgan, John 125
Morgan, Merrit W. 125-26
Morris, Mrs. 83,121
Morrow, Mr. and Mrs. Monroe 18,25
Morton, Capt. 35
Morton, Charles 10
Morton, Eleazer 9,11
Morton, Henry 10
Morton, Henry C. 9
Morton, Josephine (Stanley)
Morton, J. S. 6, 9,10,11,19, 43,45,47,111,127,134,146
Morton Memorial Home 132,146
Morton, Raymond 10
Morton, William H. 10
Moulton, Mr. 43
Moyer, Will 151
Mullen, J. W. 132
Mullen Paper Mill 132
Muskegon 48,74,78

Music 42
Myers, Lt. Chris 86-88

Napier, Ed 40-43,93,94, 96,101,121,150
Napier, Nelson 53,93
Napier, Nelson W. 42
Nelson, Arthur 137
New Buffalo 115-117,152
New York City 9,61,74,125
New York Times 61
New Richmond 26
Niles 86,117,145
Niles Weekly Mirror 40,55,93, 113
Noronic 1
Northern Michigan Transportation Co. 23,77
Northwestern Consolidated Milling Co. 30
Null, Fred H. 139
Nyack 48

Oakville 122
Ohio 123
Ongiara 16
Osborn, Arthur 134
Ottawa, Kan. 125
Overton, Glen 133
Owen, Frances Browning 140

Packards Pier 99
Palisades Park 99
Palmer, C. B. 19
Paulville 99,100,114
Paxton, James 11
Payne, L. S. 96
Pearl, Joseph F. 19,26,28,29, 46,48,53,91,106,116,131-32,135,137,147
Pearl, May (Dempster) 19,46, 106,131-32
Peatling, Rev. 143
Peck Furniture Co. 9
Peoria, Ill. 23
Pentwater 122
Pere Marquette RR 6
Pershing, Irving K. 99
Peterson Bros. 30
Petoskey 23,25,26,28,31, 32,36,54,56,58,61,63,67, 68,72,77,78,96,127,147
Pier Cove 118,151
Pierson, J. F. 79
Pierson, Sidney 67
Pike, Mrs. Jay 124
Pike's Pier 98

Pilot 96
Pipestone 133
Plummer, Timothy 39-41,102
Portland, Ore. 127
Post Boy 93
Pott, Ken 152
Protection 86-88
Pullen, Mrs. George 105
Pup 96
Puritan 13,18,121,124

Racine 73
Rand and Burger 73
Randall, J. H. 13
Reams, S. C. 132
Reed City 133
Reeve, Capt. 38
Reichle, Adolph 36
Reid's Point 62
Reid, Robert 62
Reid, R. C. 23,58,77,78, 124,147
Rensselaer, Ind. 134
Rice, M. B. 91
Rice, Rev. W. H. 138
Richard, Frank 132
Rickley, Charles 41,52,112
Ricks, Lawrence 67
Riverside 56,97,98
Roanoke 115
Robertson, W. P. 77-78
Robertson, Isaac H. 125
Robertson, Thomas 125
Robinson, Florence E. 127
Robinson, Grace E. 78
Robinson, Mrs. 151
Ross, Seward 45
Rouse, E. E. 79
Royalton Heights 8
Runyan, John 86
Russell, William 18,46,52, 54,58,120,134
Russel, Capt. Joseph 34
Ryan, John 131
Saginaw 129,130
Saginaw 127
Sahlin, Rev. George A. 138
Sailor Boy 93
Sandusky 127
Saratoga, N.Y. 121
Saugatuck 9,26,61-64,66, 68-70,90,96,101,112,113, 134,143,144,148,151
Saugatuck Commercial 63,92, 94,96,101,106,114,117,142, 143,149
Scheck, George 128

Scheck, William Miller 128
Schuler, J. S. 140
Scotland 7
Scott, Arthur O. 104
Scott, Ward 104
Seabury, Warren 133
Seasongood, Emma 128
Seymour Brothers 23
Seymour, E. W. 78
Shashaguay, Joseph 144
Shashaguay, William 143
Sheboygan, Wis. 76
Sheffield, M. H. 30
Simons, Bert 122
Simons, C. D. 50,72,117,122
Simons, Mrs. C. D. (Ollie Chadwich) 72,122
Simons, Cornelius A. 122
Simons, Del 122
Simons, J. A. 120
Simpson, Capt. and Mrs. George H. 18
Simpson, Louis Wayne 151
Sir Arthur 149
Sizelove, Charles 151-52
Skylark 11,13,121
Smith, Frank D. 143
Smith, Capt. Joe 150
Smith, Marshal 81-82
Smith, Ira A. 43,46,47,50,52, 54,112
Snyder, Will 18
Soo City 17
"A Song and a Sigh" 136
South Bend, Ind. 127,130
South Chicago 79-88,90-92
South Chicago Police Dept. 85
South Haven 13,37,39-48,50, 51,57,59,60,63,64,69,93,94, 96,101,106-108,111,112,117, 118,122,134,148,150,152
South Haven Daily Tribune 104,151
South Haven Messenger 41, 45,101,107,110
South Haven Sentinel 110, 149,150
South Haven Tribune-Messenger 120,149
Southampton, Eng. 74
Spencer, H. B. 132
Spooner, Will 41
Springsteen, Charles 18
Sprucebay 16
Sterna Milling Co. 30
Steubenville, Ohio 126

156

Stevens & Morton Lumber Co. 9
Stevensville 97
Stines, Benjamin E, 48,122,123
Stines, Edward 19,21,30,39,42,48,50,53,54,58,83,93,117,121-22,135,137,149
Stines, Mrs. Edward 47,48,69
Stines, Henry 36,73-76,122
St. Joseph 1,6-9,11-13,17,18,20,21,23,26,27,29,31-36,38,48,50,53,54,63,67,68,72,75,76,79,86,93,96,98,105,114,117,118,120-126,128,131-33,135,136,147,149,150
St. Joseph & Lake Michigan Transportation Co. 17
St. Joseph Daily News 52,121
St. Joseph Hotel Co. 6
St. Joseph Life Saving Station 23
St. Joseph Press 43
St. Joseph Saturday Herald 17,23,77
St. Louis, Mo. 23,130
Stone, Melville E. 110
Stratton, Sheriff Joseph 113,114
Strickland, E. F. 66
Sunlight Center Club 151
Swick, Bill 101

Tacoma, Wash. 127

Tarbell, Grosvenor 26
Terre Haute, Ind. 23,48
"The Rime of the Ancient Mariner" 29
Three Oaks 32
Three Oaks Press 26,57,92,96,115,116.117,132,142
Tibbits, Mr. 46
Toledo & Ann Arbor No. 2 78
Tramp 25,32,35,52,54,72,77,98
Tri-Cities Museum 148

U. S. Hydrographic Bureau 44
Umphrey, Simon Frank 57
Union Banking Co. 6
Upper Sandusky, Ohio 128

Vandalia RR 18,23,48
Vandervere, Mr. 98
Vanderveer, Mr. 98
Vargo, George 120
Varney, Frank 67
Virginia 73

Wade, President 143
Warrenko 16
Wart, G. M. 116
Washburn-Crosby Milling Co. 30
Waterman, Nixon 135,136,137

Waters, Richard 22
Watervliet 98
Weckler, Adam 52
Wells, Henry 106,107
Werner, John 26
Werner, John A. 129
West Bay City 13
Western Indiana RR 8
Wheeler, F. W. & Co. 13
Whistler, G. S. 30,73-76
Whiting, Ind. 81,84,85,92
Wilcox, C. B. 126
Williams, Del 102
Williams, H. W. 11, 13
Williams, H. W. 43
Williams, John 90
Willoughby, Ohio 127
Wilson, Mrs. Kate M. B. 137
Wirtz, Alfred 108,128
Wirtz, Mr. and Mrs. Frank 127
Wolseley, Garnet 15
Wood, Will 133
Woodcock, E. F. 86
Worden, Ed 107
"Wreck of the Chicora" 141-42
Wright, John 82
Wyman, Pearl 105

Yakes, J. W. 74
Yendes, Mrs. H. W. 126

* * *

Kit Lane, a Michigan native, graduated from Michigan State University and received an MLS degree from Western Michigan University. She and her husband, Art, are former owners of the *Commercial Record* and *Fennville Herald* weekly newspapers in western Allegan County. Other newspaper work includes stints with the *Detroit Free Press, Grand Rapids Press, Birmingham Eccentric* and *Daily Tribune* of Royal Oak. In addition to a number of books on Saugatuck area history, and the first two volumes of the Saugatuck Maritime Series, she is the author of *Lucius Lyon: An Eminently Useful Citizen* and *John Allen: Michigan's Pioneer Promoter*. Kit is also a frequent speaker on such topics as early Michigan history, genealogy and the state's Victorian poets. The Lanes live in Douglas, near Lake Michigan, not far from where the masts of the **Chicora** came ashore in 1895.

Illustration Credits

p. 7,121,122,123,124,135,126,127,130,131: Memorial Poster at Tri-Cities Museum, Grand Haven, Michigan

p.8: *A Twentieth Century History of Berrien County* by Judge Orville Coolidge (Lewis Publishing Co.: Chicago) 1906.

p. 10,14,29,58,74: Institute for Great Lakes Research, Bowling Green State University, Perrysburg, Ohio.

p. 12,27: Benton Harbor Library, Sanborn Fire map collection.

p. 19,95: National Archives

p. 21: Michigan Maritime Museum, South Haven

p. 34: Drawn by Ann G. Gray from an old photograph.

p. 41,62: *Illustrated Atlas of Allegan County, Michigan* (The Kace Publishing Co.: Racine, Wis.) 1895.

p. 49: Leaf from Graham & Morton Co. minute book in the Michigan Archives and Regional Collection, Western Michigan University, Kalamazoo.

p. 109,113,144,148: Allegan County Historical Society Museum, Allegan

p. 143: Jeanne Hallgren

p. 152: C. Patrick Labadie

Sources and Acknowledgments

Libraries, most with newspaper collections: New Buffalo Public Library; Maude Preston Palenske Library, St. Joseph; Milwaukee Public Library; Benton Harbor Public Library; Herrick Public Library, Holland; Michigan City Public Library, Michigan City, Indiana; Three Oaks Township Library; Allegan Public Library; Loutit Library, Grand Haven; Grand Rapids Public Library; Chicago Historical Society Library; Library of Michigan, Lansing; South Haven Public Library; files of the Saugatuck *Commercial Record* and *Fennville Herald*; and the newspaper collections of the Manistee Museum.

Other sources consulted include: Scrapbooks compiled by Jeannette Stieve, now in the Marialyce Canonie Library of the Michigan Maritime Museum library, South Haven; business records of Graham & Morton at the Western Michigan Regional Collection and Archives, Western Michigan University, Kalamazoo; ships' plans from the Detroit Drydock Co. in the Institute for Great Lakes Research, Bowling Green University, Perrysburg, Ohio.

Thanks also for assistance by individuals including: the late Nellie (Bryan) Howlett, Douglas; C. Patrick Labadie of the Canal Park Museum, Duluth, Minnesota; Ken Pott of the Michigan Maritime Museum, South Haven; Steve Harold of the Manistee Museum, Marguerite Miller at the Allegan County Historical Society Museum, Allegan; John Pahl, Allegan; and the curator and staff of the Tri-Cities Museum, Grand Haven.

Saugatuck
Maritime Series

Built on the Banks of the Kalamazoo

Book 1 covers boats built on the Kalamazoo River in southwestern Michigan from Indian canoes to today's championship racing boats. The riverbank has also been the construction site for plank river rafts, white oak schooners, tug boats, steam freight and passenger craft and, in more recent years, steel paddle wheel excursion boats, flat-bottomed houseboats and luxury aluminum yachts. This volume covers boat construction at Saugatuck and Douglas near the mouth of the river, as well as Allegan, New Richmond, Kalamazoo, Marshall and Albion farther upstream. The life histories of more than 200 vessels are traced, profusely illustrated.

"The Dustless Road to Happyland" Chicago-Saugatuck Passenger Boats 1859-1929

Book 2 tells the story of passenger traffic between the mouth of the Kalamazoo and Chicago beginning with the Goodrich-owned steamer **Huron** in 1859 through the Goodrich Transit Company boats that maintained service until 1929. Saugatuck was also a base of operation for the Crawford Transportation Co., the Indiana Transportation Co. (until service stopped abruptly the week the **Eastland** capsized in 1915) and the boats of Graham & Morton. Also included in this volume is an account of the years that the **North American** and the **South American** of the Georgian Bay Line used Saugatuck as a winter harbor, the history of the chain ferry across the Kalamazoo River, the museum ship **Keewatin** and a summary of commercial and sport fishing in the river and nearby Lake Michigan.

Chicora Lost on Lake Michigan

Book 3 relates the story of the day, January 21, 1895, that the **Chicora**, Graham & Morton Company's newest and finest steamer, disappeared on a routine winter trip from Milwaukee to St. Joseph. When wreckage began to come ashore at South Haven and Saugatuck the worst fears were confirmed. Then began the search for the sunken hull, a quest that has continued for a century.

Book 4 will focus on boats that have been wrecked on southeastern Lake Michigan.

Also Available from PAVILION PRESS:

The Wreck of the Hippocampus and Other Tales of Saugatuck

Stories of the Saugatuck area including the rescue of survivors of the **Hippocampus** in 1868, the romance of Mt. Baldhead and a description of the 20th Century steamer **Anna C. Wilson**. The day the Big Pavilion burned in 1960 is also vividly recalled.

The Letters of William G. Butler and Other Tales of Saugatuck

Letters written by Allegan County's first settler, 1833 to 1842, a journal of an around-the-world trip taken in 1869 by George N. Dutcher, son of the founder of Douglas, an account of a duel on the banks of the Kalamazoo, the history of the cannon in Saugatuck's village square and more.

The Popcorn Millionaire and Other Tales of Saugatuck

Famous residents and visitors including D. K. Ludwig, former popcorn vendor, who was the richest man in the worl in 1976, suffragette Susan B. Anthony, architect George W. Maher, poet Carl Sandburg, Amelia Earhart, Robby Benson, Paderewski and others.

The Day the Elephant Died and Other Tales of Saugatuck

True stories, or nearly so, of sunken gold during the state's wildcat banking era, Michigan soldiers during the Civil War, battling the Air Force for possession of the Saugatuck's radar dome, and, of course, the day the elephant died.

Buried Singapore: Michigan's Imaginary Pompeii

A history of the buried town of Singapore, near the mouth of the Kalamazoo River. The first sawmill was built there in 1837 and one or more mills operated most of the time until 1875 when the last saw was packed aboard a boat and taken north to begin work in the forests of the Upper Peninsula. Most of the buildings of Singapore were carried off to do service elsewhere, and what little that was left was gradually buried beneath the sand.

Lucius Lyon: An Eminently Useful Citizen

Early surveyor, territorial delegate, a leader at Michigan's Constitutional Convention in 1835, the state's first senator, and founder of Kalamazoo, Grand Rapids, Schoolcraft and other communities. A moving force in Michigan from 1822 to his death in 1851.

By Kit Lane

And more, for a free catalog write:

PAVILION PRESS P.O. Box 250, Douglas, MI 49406